ENVIRONMENTAL LAW

Second Edition

by
Margaret C. Jasper

Oceana's Legal Almanac Series:
Law for the Layperson

2002
Oceana Publications, Inc.
Dobbs Ferry, New York

Information contained in this work has been obtained by Oceana Publications from sources believed to be reliable. However, neither the Publisher nor its authors guarantee the accuracy or completeness of any information published herein, and neither Oceana nor its authors shall be responsible for any errors, omissions or damages arising from the use of this information. This work is published with the understanding that Oceana and its authors are supplying information, but are not attempting to render legal or other professional services. If such services are required, the assistance of an appropriate professional should be sought.

Library of Congress Control Number 2002101425

ISBN: 0-379-11364-3

Oceana's Legal Almanac Series: Law for the Layperson
ISSN 1075-7376

©2002 by Oceana Publications, Inc.

To My Husband Chris

Your love and support
are my motivation and inspiration

-and-

In memory of my son, Jimmy

Table of Contents

CHAPTER 4:
WATER QUALITY

CHAPTER 5:
HAZARDOUS MATERIALS AND SOLID WASTES

CHAPTER 6:
BIODIVERSITY CONSERVATION

CHAPTER 7:
ENDANGERED SPECIES

ABOUT THE AUTHOR

MARGARET C. JASPER is an attorney engaged in the general practice of law in South Salem, New York, concentrating in the areas of personal injury and entertainment law. Ms. Jasper holds a Juris Doctor degree from Pace University School of Law, White Plains, New York, is a member of the New York and Connecticut bars, and is certified to practice before the United States District Courts for the Southern and Eastern Districts of New York, the United States Court of Appeals for the Second Circuit, and the United States Supreme Court.

Ms. Jasper has been appointed to the panel of arbitrators of the American Arbitration Association and the law guardian panel for the Family Court of the State of New York, is a member of the Association of Trial Lawyers of America, and is a New York State licensed real estate broker and member of the Westchester County Board of Realtors, operating as Jasper Real Estate, in South Salem, New York. Margaret Jasper maintains a website at http://members.aol.com/JasperLaw.

Ms. Jasper is the author and general editor of the following legal almanacs: Juvenile Justice and Children's Law; Marriage and Divorce; Estate Planning; The Law of Contracts; The Law of Dispute Resolution; Law for the Small Business Owner; The Law of Personal Injury; Real Estate Law for the Homeowner and Broker; Everyday Legal Forms; Dictionary of Selected Legal Terms; The Law of Medical Malpractice; The Law of Product Liability; The Law of No-Fault Insurance; The Law of Immigration; The Law of Libel and Slander; The Law of Buying and Selling; Elder Law; The Right to Die; AIDS Law; The Law of Obscenity and Pornography; The Law of Child Custody; The Law of Debt Collection; Consumer Rights Law; Bankruptcy Law for the Individual Debtor; Victim's Rights Law; Animal Rights Law; Workers' Compensation Law; Employee Rights in the Workplace; Probate Law; Environmental Law; Labor Law; The Americans with Disabilities Act; The Law of Capital Punishment; Education Law; The Law of Violence Against Women; Landlord-Tenant

Law; Insurance Law; Religion and the Law; Commercial Law; Motor Vehicle Law; Social Security Law; The Law of Drunk Driving; The Law of Speech and the First Amendment; Employment Discrimination Under Title VII; Hospital Liability Law; Home Mortgage Law Primer; Copyright Law; Patent Law; Trademark Law; Special Education Law; The Law of Attachment and Garnishment; Banks and their Customers; and Credit Cards and the Law.

INTRODUCTION

The health of our environment—the world in which we live—depends upon how we treat it. Our personal health very much depends upon the health of our environment. In other words, we need each other. The cleanliness and safety of the air we breathe and the water we drink are directly related to how well we safeguard our world. Mistreatment and neglect of our environment—by both individuals and industry—will come back to haunt us in the future, for generations to come.

We have already witnessed the pollution of our waterways and our air. Rivers which were once great sources of fishing and recreational activities have become polluted, acidic pools of useless water. Decades of discharging chemicals into the atmosphere has made it nearly dangerous to breathe in many areas of the country.

As society becomes more aware of the harmful effects of a polluted environment, there is growing concern over rehabilitating and protecting our natural resources. Individuals are concerned that the air they breathe and the water they drink is kept clean and safe. They are concerned that the food they eat is free from contaminants and that the benefits of balanced plant and wildlife systems are restored and preserved. They want their children to grow up in a safe and healthy environment.

Due to the growing public awareness, the average person has become more involved with environmental issues and is familiar with such terms as acid rain, ozone depletion, global warming, secondhand smoke, UV rays, asbestos contamination, rainforests and wetlands, and their impact on our environment. Even elementary schools routinely include environmental studies as part of their science curriculum.

A table of acronyms and abbreviations related to environmental issues is set forth at Appendix 1.

Prior to the enactment of the sweeping federal environmental statutes discussed in this almanac, there have historically been common law remedies for a variety of environmental concerns. For example, the common law doctrine of "riparian rights" refers to the privileges enjoyed by landowners in connection with the waterways which flow through their property. Under the common law doctrine of "public nuisance," it is illegal to cause or permit a condition to exist which injures or endangers the public health, safety or welfare. Similarly, under the common law doctrine of "private nuisance," it is illegal to destroy or deteriorate an individual's property, or interfere with an individual's lawful use or enjoyment of their property.

Nevertheless, the most significant environmental legislation has been enacted in the past several decades when Congress began to enact statutes dealing with specific environmental issues, such as the Clean Air Act to address air quality, and the Clean Water Act to address water quality. Although in enacting legislation governing these environmental concerns, Congress preempted jurisdiction over these areas, it provided that state and local governments could enact similar environmental protection legislation as long as those standards were equal to or stricter than the federal standards.

As a result of these federal, state and local environmental statutes and restrictions, the practice of environmental law is rapidly expanding. Lawyers are frequently hired to represent parties in a wide array of environmental matters. Legal assistance is needed to provide guidance to clients in complying with certain statutory mandates. For example, land developers are concerned about land use legalities, such as building in wetland areas, and seek legal advice to ensure that they proceed according to environmental statutes.

In addition, statutes such as the Clean Air Act allows private citizens the right to bring a citizen suit for penalties against a source of pollution—or the government—if the law is not enforced. Many environmentalist groups have taken advantage of this right to bring about compliance with the environmental statutes.

This almanac presents an overview of environmental law, including a general discussion of important environmental issues, including air and water quality, hazardous materials and wastes, wetlands preservation, and endangered species. This almanac also explores the effects these pollutants have on our health and on the health of our children, who are a particularly vulnerable risk group.

This almanac also discusses and defines the role of the United States Environmental Protection Agency and its subdivisions in enforcing the legislation and carrying out the national objective of safeguarding the environment.

The Appendix provides the text of applicable statutes, directories of relevant agencies, and other pertinent information and data. The Glossary contains definitions of many of the terms used throughout the almanac.

CHAPTER 1:
THE ENVIRONMENTAL PROTECTION AGENCY

IN GENERAL

The United States Environmental Protection Agency (EPA) is the federal agency responsible for protecting public health from environmental problems. This is accomplished in large part by improving the natural environment upon which human life depends, e.g the air, land and water. The EPA is comprised of a number of subdivisions which handle specific environmental issues and problems. The EPA ensures that the federal environmental laws are implemented and enforced.

A directory of regional EPA offices is set forth at Appendix 2.

THE OFFICE OF ENFORCEMENT AND COMPLIANCE ASSURANCE

Complying with environmental regulations is important in protecting public health and the environment. The EPA is responsible for enforcing and assuring compliance with environmental regulations. In enforcing the law, the EPA has collected the largest penalties ever from those who pollute the air, the water, and the land in violation of the law.

The EPA's Office of Enforcement and Compliance Assurance (OECA) is responsible for making sure those subject to regulation are in compliance with the law. In order to do so, the OECA assists businesses and communities with compliance training and guidance and uses regulatory enforcement tactics.

Compliance Assistance

The OECA has established national Compliance Assistance Centers for specific industries heavily populated with small businesses and entities that face substantial federal regulation. These industries include: printing, metal finishing, automotive services and repair, printed wiring boards, small chemical manufacturers and agriculture.

The purpose of the centers is to provide comprehensive, easy to understand compliance information—such as plain-language guides, checklists and fact sheets, etc.—targeted specifically to those industries set forth below.

CCAR-GreenLink

This Center helps the automotive service and repair community identify flexible, common sense ways to comply with environmental requirements.

National Metal Finishing Resource Center

This Center provides comprehensive environmental compliance, technical assistance, and pollution prevention information to the metal finishing industry.

ChemAlliance

This Center provides innovative website features to direct chemical manufacturers to information resources and plain-language compliance assistance material.

Paints and Coatings Resource Center

This Center provides regulatory compliance and pollution prevention information to organic coating facilities, industry vendors and suppliers, and others.

Federal Facilities Compliance Assistance Center

This Center provides information about environmental laws and regulations that affect Federal departments and agencies.

Printed Wiring Board Resource Center

This Center provides regulatory compliance and pollution prevention information to printed wiring board manufacturers, industry vendors and suppliers, and others.

Local Government Environmental Assistance Network

This Center provides environmental management, planning, and regulatory information for local government officials, managers, and staff.

Printers' National Environmental Assistance Center

This Center offers training, state regulatory compliance guides, and two e-mail discussion groups on technical and regulatory issues.

National Agriculture Compliance Assistance Center

This Center offers comprehensive easy-to-understand information on environmentally protective and agriculturally sound approaches to compliance.

Transportation Environmental Resource Center

This Center provides compliance assistance information for each mode of transportation—air, shipping and barging, rail, and trucking.

Regulatory Enforcement

The regulatory enforcement programs are administered through OECA subdivisions, which are responsible for developing enforcement policies, and bringing civil or criminal enforcement actions.

The Air Enforcement Division

The Air Enforcement Division (AED) is responsible for judicial and administrative enforcement activities under the Clean Air Act, including the 1990 Amendments to the Act; and the Noise Control Act. The AED's Mobile Source Program enforces national motor vehicle fuel and emissions standards. The Stationary Source Program oversees woodstoves, acid rain, and stratospheric ozone protection.

The AED provides technical, scientific and engineering support; participates in and manages case negotiations; prepares litigation and settlement documents; and presents federal cases in administrative and court proceedings, including administrative or judicial appeals. The AED is the primary authority on all enforcement aspects of programs related to the Clean Air Act, and is primarily responsible for enforcement-related rulemaking. In addition, the AED is responsible for reviewing Citizen Suits and amicus briefs submitted pursuant to the Clean Air Act.

The Water Enforcement Division

The Water Enforcement Division (WED) is responsible for The Clean Water Act, the Safe Drinking Water Act, the Marine Protection, Research, and Sanctuaries Act, and the Oil Pollution Act. The WED also reviews citizen enforcement actions; participates in regulatory development and interpretation; and develops national enforcement policies.

The WED works closely with other OECA offices, the EPA's Office of Water, the EPA's Office of General Counsel, its Regional Offices, the States, and the Department of Justice on water enforcement matters.

Hazardous Wastes and the Resource Conservation and Recovery Act Enforcement Division

Pursuant to the Resource Conservation and Recovery Act (RCRA), the role of the Resource Conservation and Recovery Act Enforcement Division is to oversee the national hazardous waste enforcement program. They are responsible for protecting citizens from unacceptably high health risks caused by hazardous wastes. They also serve as a national clearinghouse for legal and technical advice, information, and data, so as to bring the industry into compliance. This division takes enforcement action against and prosecutes violators, and oversees administrative and judicial appellate litigation.

The Toxics and Pesticides Enforcement Division

The Toxics and Pesticides Enforcement Division (TPED) handles case development, policy and enforcement issues pursuant to the Federal Insecticide, Fungicide, and Rodenticide Act, the Toxic Substances Control Act, and the Emergency Planning and Community Right-to-Know Act.

The responsibilities of the TPED include: (i) coordination of national enforcement case initiatives; (ii) development of nationally significant cases; (iii) development of toxics and pesticides policy/guidance documents affecting case development and litigation; (iv) participation in regulatory workgroups; (v) promotion of supplemental environmental projects; (vi) providing support to the regions and the states on regional and state cases; (vii) maintaining liaison with the criminal office; (viii) undertaking legislative work; (ix) pursuing case development training; and (x) coordination of these activities with the states, OECA, the Department of Justice, and other concerned federal agencies.

The Multimedia Enforcement Division

The Multimedia Enforcement Division (MED) coordinates existing multimedia enforcement programs nationwide and promotes these programs at the state and regional level. The MED provides legal and technical support for enforcement activities, coordination for national cases, contractual support for case development, and serves as an information clearinghouse for multimedia enforcement issues.

The MED coordinates enforcement efforts against companies who have violations at multiple facilities, revises EPA guidance documents, and improves coordination of penalty policies across different media programs. Multimedia enforcement is integral to the EPA's mandate to protect human health and the nation's environment.

The Federal Facilities Enforcement Office

The Federal Facilities Enforcement Office (FFEO) is responsible for making sure that Federal facilities take actions necessary to prevent, control, and abate environmental pollution. The FFEO is composed of two groups: (i) the Site Remediation and Enforcement Staff; and (ii) the Planning, Prevention and Compliance Staff. These two groups help to develop national policy and guidance related to compliance and enforcement issues confronting Federal facilities.

The National Enforcement Investigations Center

The National Enforcement Investigations Center (NEIC) employs scientists, engineers, analysts, computer specialists, and environmental specialists who conduct field investigations associated with highly complex technical and regulatory pollution problems that impact human health and the environment. The NEIC laboratory is a recognized center of expertise in forensic environmental chemistry. The Center has established a reputation for providing laboratory analyses of the type and quality needed to support complex and unusual enforcement efforts.

NEIC specialists assess, organize, and analyze information in order to prepare for investigations, settlements, negotiations, and trials. The NEIC provides expert analysis of a regulated entity's financial records to determine its ability to pay proposed fines and/or cleanup costs. Cost recovery activities include research of corporate structures, investigation into corporate and individual finances, and tracking unreported corporate or individual finances.

NEIC experts advise EPA headquarters, regional offices, Department of Justice and U.S. Attorneys' offices regarding technical, regulatory, and financial issues that arise during case development, settlement negotiations, and litigation. NEIC personnel frequently serve as expert and fact witnesses during civil and criminal legal proceedings. NEIC procedures, data, and information are developed to withstand rigorous legal and scientific scrutiny.

The Criminal Investigations Division

The Criminal Investigations Division (CID) is responsible for criminal enforcement of the federal environmental statutes. The CID investigates the most serious and willful polluters who pose the greatest threat to human health and the environment. The CID also provides training to its employees and partners. There are approximately 178 special agents employed by the CID nationwide and participates nationwide in a multitude of environmental crime task forces. Its partners in these task forces consist of other federal law enforcement agencies, the U.S. Attorney's office, as well as state and local law enforcement and environmental agencies.

A Directory of Regional EPA Criminal Investigations Division Offices is set forth at Appendix 3.

THE OFFICE OF ADMINISTRATIVE LAW JUDGES

The EPA's Office of Administrative Law Judges (OALJ) is an independent office in the Office of the Administrator of the EPA. The Administrative Law Judges conduct hearings and render decisions in proceedings between the EPA and persons, businesses, government entities, and other organizations which are or are alleged to be regulated under environmental laws.

Administrative Law Judges preside in enforcement and permit proceedings under the Administrative Procedure Act and in other proceedings involving alleged violations of environmental statutes. Most enforcement actions initiated by the EPA are for the assessment of civil penalties.

The environmental statutes under which proceedings are brought before the Administrative Law Judges include:

1. The Clean Air Act

2. The Clean Water Act

3. The Comprehensive Environmental Response, Compensation and Liability Act

4. The Emergency Planning and Community Right-To-Know Act

5. The Federal Insecticide, Fungicide, and Rodenticide Act

6. The Marine Protection, Research and Sanctuaries Act

7. The Safe Drinking Water Act

8. The Solid Waste Disposal Act (as amended by the Resource Conservation and Recovery Act)

9. The Toxic Substances Control Act; and

10. The Asbestos Hazard Emergency Response Act

All decisions issued by the Administrative Law Judges are subject to review by the Environmental Appeals Board (EAB). The Administrative Law Judge's initial decision, which is a disposition of all of the issues in a proceeding, becomes the final order of the EPA within 45 days after service upon the parties unless a party appeals to the EAB or the EAB on its own initiative elects to review the initial decision.

THE ENVIRONMENTAL APPEALS BOARD

The Environmental Appeals Board (EAB) consists of four Environmental Appeals Judges appointed by the Administrator. The EAB is the final decisionmaker on administrative appeals under all major environmental statutes that the EPA administers. It is an impartial and independent body created in 1992 in recognition of the growing importance of EPA adjudicatory proceedings as a mechanism for implementing and enforcing the environmental laws.

The EAB's caseload consists primarily of appeals from permit decisions and civil penalty decisions. The EAB also hears petitions for reimbursement of costs incurred in complying with cleanup orders issued under the Comprehensive Environmental Response, Compensation, and Liability Act of 1980 (CERCLA).

The EAB sits in panels of three and decides each matter by majority vote. Decisions of the Board are final and may not be further appealed to the Administrator. However, the parties may have statutory rights of appeal to federal court under the various environmental statutes.

EPA COMPLAINT HOTLINES

Individuals who have tips or complaints concerning an environmental matter are advised to contact their local or state environmental agency, or one of the EPA's departmental hotlines.

A Directory of EPA departmental hotlines is set forth at Appendix 4.

CHAPTER 2:
OUTDOOR AIR QUALITY

IN GENERAL

All Americans are concerned that the air they breathe is clean and healthy. Air pollution can make your eyes, nose and throat burn. More significantly, some chemicals that have been released into the air have been linked to cancer, brain damage, nerve damage, birth defects and serious respiratory illness. In fact, some air pollutants may even cause death.

Air pollution also adversely affects the environment. It has damaged and destroyed foliage and harmed animals. Air pollution has damaged the ozone layer which protects the Earth from harmful rays. This in turn can cause illnesses, such as skin cancer and cataracts. Air pollution also destroys property. For example, it erodes stone, dirties property, and can cause a dangerous visibility-reducing haze.

MAJOR OUTDOOR AIR POLLUTANTS

There are six major outdoor air pollutants for which the EPA has set national standards: (i) ozone; (ii) particulate matter; (iii) carbon monoxide; (iv) lead; (v) nitrogen dioxide; and (vi) sulfur dioxide.

Ozone

There are two types of ozone. One is good—ozone in the stratosphere, and the other is bad—ozone at ground-level. Ground-level ozone is formed by the chemical reaction of pollutants from cars, trucks, and buses, chemical plants, refineries, power plants, other combustion activities and factories. Ozone is the principal ingredient of smog.

More people are exposed to ozone than any other outdoor air pollutant. Even low levels of ozone exposure have been linked to respiratory problems and reduced lung functioning. Ozone pollution is greatest in the summer.

Particulate Matter

Particulate matter includes dust, dirt, soot, smoke and liquid droplets directly emitted into the air by sources such as factories, power plants, cars, construction activity, fires and natural windblown dust.

Carbon Monoxide

Carbon monoxide is formed when carbon in fuels is not completely burned. It is a colorless, odorless gas, and at high levels it can be poisonous. Motor vehicle exhaust contributes 60% of all carbon monoxide emissions and as much as 95% of the carbon monoxide in the air may come from automobile exhaust. Carbon monoxide enters the bloodstream through the lungs and reduces oxygen delivery to organs and tissues. Visual impairment, reduced manual dexterity, poor learning ability, reduced work capacity, difficulty in performing complex tasks are associated with outdoor exposure to high levels of carbon monoxide.

Lead

In addition to the lead exposure found indoors, lead is also found in the air, soil, and water and it can be inhaled or ingested. Outdoor lead exposure is a national health concern. Fortunately, the removal of lead from gasoline has dramatically reduced outdoor lead pollution.

Nitrogen Dioxide

Nitrogen dioxide is a reddish brown, highly reactive gas formed in the atmosphere through the oxidation of nitrogen oxides. Outdoor sources of nitrogen dioxide include automobiles and power plants. Short-term exposures to nitrogen dioxide—e.g., less than 3 hours—may produce changes in airway responsiveness and pulmonary function. Long-term exposure may lead to increased susceptibility to respiratory infection and may cause alteration in the lungs.

Sulfur Dioxide

Sulfur dioxide is formed when coal or oil fuel containing sulfur is burned. Short-term exposure to sulfur dioxide may result in reduced lung function and symptoms of wheezing, chest tightness, or shortness of breath. Long-term exposure may cause respiratory illness.

A chart of common air pollutants is set forth at Appendix 5.

THE AIR QUALITY INDEX

The Air Quality Index groups pollutant levels into 6 categories: (i) good; (ii) moderate; (iii) unhealthy for sensitive groups; (iv) unhealthy; (v) very unhealthy; and (vi)hazardous. For each of these groupings and for each pollutant, cautionary statements concerning certain segments of the population, (e.g., children, people with respiratory disease, the elderly, etc.) are provided, indicating whether to limit time or activity outdoors.

For example, If ozone is in the air quality index category "unhealthy for sensitive groups" the cautionary statement is: "Active children and adults, and people with respiratory disease, such as asthma, should limit heavy outdoor exertion." Limiting outdoor exercise is important because exercise increases the likelihood of breathing through the mouth, rather than the nose, which can filter half of the ozone. Thus, pollution that would normally be filtered through the nose goes straight to the lungs.

The air quality index may be found in the local paper, TV, or radio, or may be obtained from the local and state air pollution control agencies. A directory of state and local air pollution control agencies may be obtained by visiting the following website: http://www.4cleanair.org.

To find out what air pollutants are common in your area, and to discover what is causing the pollution, the reader can visit The Environmental Defense Fund website at http://www.scorecard.org, or the EPA's Airnow website at http://www.epa.gov/airnow.

THE CLEAN AIR ACT (42 U.S.C. 7401 ET SEQ.)

Improving and protecting the quality of our air is a national goal which requires the cooperation and efforts of many agencies, organizations, industries, as well as the public. The primary source of legislation designed to improve air quality is the Clean Air Act, enacted by Congress in 1970. Major changes to the original Act were made with the passage of The 1990 Clean Air Act Amendments—the most recent version of the law.

The 1990 Clean Air Act is a comprehensive statute which attempts to address all aspects of the complex problem of air pollution. It contains seven separate titles covering different regulatory programs. The term Clean Air Act as used in this almanac refers to the 1990 Clean Air Act.

As further discussed below, the Clean Air Act covers some of the most pressing environmental problems facing Americans today, such as acid rain, toxic air emissions and urban air pollution. In addition, the Act established a national permit program, and strengthened enforcement capabilities.

State Involvement

Although the 1990 Clean Air Act is a federal law, the states carry much responsibility in administering the Act. The law recognizes that solving pollution problems in various areas often requires a special understanding of the local area, including its geography and industry. To assist the states in developing successful clean air programs, the EPA provides funding, and services, e.g., scientific research and engineering services.

The Act sets a maximum threshold on how much of a pollutant can be in the air. This standard applies to the entire country to ensure that all individuals have the same basic health and environmental protections. Nevertheless, the individual states are permitted to have their own air pollution laws, provided their standards are equal to or more stringent than the federal law.

It is an established fact that air pollution can travel across state borders. Thus, the Clean Air Act includes provisions designed to reduce interstate air pollution, and provides for interstate commissions on air pollution control. These commissions are responsible for developing regional strategies for cleaning up air pollution.

Of course, air pollution can also move across national borders. The Clean Air Act addresses that problem as well, and includes provisions designed to reduce pollution that originates in Mexico and Canada and drifts into the United States, as well as pollution from the United States that extends to Canada and Mexico.

Title I: Air Pollution Prevention and Control

Title I of the Clean Air Act is concerned with air pollution prevention and control. The task of keeping our air clean, and cleaning air that has become dirty, is the responsibility of the U.S. EPA's Office of Air Quality Planning & Standards (OAQPS). The OAQPS carries out their responsibilities by collecting data, undertaking research and analysis, and enforcing air quality standards. The Clean Air Act provides the regulatory framework within which the OAQPS operates.

As set forth above, there are six "criteria pollutants" established as indicators of air quality. These pollutants are commonly found all over the country, and are known to cause harm to health, and damage to the environment and property.—The OAQPS has further established a maximum concentration of these criteria pollutants. The OAQPS monitors air quality standards by measuring concentrations of criteria pollutants. These measurements are taken at nationwide monitoring stations. Any levels above the established maximum concentration are deemed to have adverse effects on human health.

One set of limits—known as the primary standard—protects health. Any levels above the established maximum concentration limits are deemed to have adverse effects on human health. Another set of limits—known as the secondary standard—addresses environmental and property damage.

These maximum limits are known as National Ambient Air Quality Standards (NAAQS). A geographic area that meets or does better than the National Ambient Air Quality Standard is called an attainment area. If an area does not meet this standard, it is called a nonattainment area. It has been estimated that about 90 million Americans live in nonattainment areas.

Under the Act, each state is required to develop a written plan for cleaning the air in their areas. This plan, called a State Implementation Plan (SIP), sets forth the steps the state is going to take to improve air quality and to keep clean air from deteriorating. The states must involve the public, through hearings and opportunities to comment, in the development of each state implementation plan.

The SIP must be approved by the EPA. If a state fails to develop an acceptable plan, the EPA is entitled to take jurisdiction over enforcement of the Clean Air Act for that state.

On an annual basis, the EPA examines the air pollution trends of the six criteria pollutants and releases a document setting forth a detailed analysis of changes in air pollution levels over the last 10 years time, plus a summary of the current air pollution status. This document is known as the National Air Quality and Emissions Trends Report.

Title II: National Emissions Standards—Mobile Sources of Pollution

Title II of the Clean Air Act is concerned with the emissions standards for mobile sources of air pollution. A mobile source is one which is able to move, e.g. cars, trucks, and buses. These vehicles emit large amounts of hazardous pollutants into the air, and are the primary source of the urban smog problem.

Smog consists of ground-level ozone. Although ozone located high above the earth protects us, ground-level ozone is harmful. Ground-level ozone is produced by the combination of hazardous pollutants, including exhaust fumes.

Smog forms as the pollutants are blown through the air by the wind. Because the wind blows the smog-forming pollutants away from their sources, smog may be more severe far away from the source.

Smog forms more easily when it is hot and sunny. The pollutants literally "cook" in the air. The severity of smog depends very much on the weather and geographical factors. For example, when warm air stays near the ground instead of rising—known as a temperature inversion—and winds are calm, smog may remain for days.

Efforts to produce cleaner fuels and engines, and to make sure that pollution control devices operate efficiently, are expected to reduce hazardous air pollutants from mobile sources. In fact, cars today produce up to 80 percent less pollution than in the 1960's.

For the most part, leaded gasoline has been discontinued, causing a significant decline in air levels of the toxic chemical. Nevertheless, motor vehicles are still responsible for up to half of the smog-forming VOCs and nitrogen oxides (NOx), releasing more than 50 percent of the hazardous air pollutants, and up to 90 percent of the carbon monoxide found in urban air.

To address this problem, the Clean Air Act has endeavored to reduce the pollution caused by motor vehicles. The law calls for using cleaner cars and fuels and requiring auto inspections to make sure automobiles are maintained.

In order to make a significant dent in automobile pollution, cleaner fuels must be developed. Under the Clean Air Act, gasoline refiners must reformulate the gasoline sold in the smoggiest areas so it contains less volatile organic compounds (VOCs), such as benzene—a hazardous air pollutant that causes cancer and aplastic anemia.

To combat carbon monoxide pollution in certain areas, refiners will have to sell oxyfuel, gasoline with oxygen added to make the fuel burn more efficiently, thereby reducing carbon monoxide release. Further, all gasolines will have to contain detergents to keep engines working smoothly and burning fuel cleanly. The Clean Air Act also encourages the development of alternative fuels such as alcohols, liquefied petroleum gas, and natural gas.

The Clean Air Act requires car manufacturers to build a certain number of cars which use cleaner fuels, and electric cars, which are low in pollution. The law also requires cars to have under-the-hood systems and dashboard warning lights that check whether pollution control devices are working properly. The law extends the working life of these pollution control devices from 50,000 miles to 100,000 miles.

Smaller trucks are subject to similar requirements as automobiles. Large diesel trucks and buses are required to be manufactured in such a way as to reduce particulate releases by at least 90 percent.

In addition to cleaner fuels and cars, the law also requires that vehicles undergo periodic inspection and maintenance to makes sure the pollution emissions are kept at a low level.

Title III: Toxic Air Pollutants

Title III of the Clean Air Act is concerned with toxic air pollutants. According to the EPA, more than 2.7 billion pounds of toxic air pollutants are emitted annually in the United States, and such exposure has been linked to 1000 to 3000 cancer deaths each year. Toxic air pollutants have also been linked with the destruction of the protective ozone layer.

To remedy this problem, the Act sets forth a list of 189 hazardous air pollutants selected by Congress on the basis of potential health and/or environmental hazard. The EPA is required to regulate these listed air toxics. The EPA is also permitted to add new chemicals to the list as it deems necessary.

To regulate hazardous air pollutants, the EPA must identify categories of sources that release the 189 chemicals listed by Congress, such as gas stations, chemical plants, etc. The air toxics producers are further classified as either large or small sources.

Once the categories of sources are listed, the EPA issues regulations, in some cases setting forth exact specifications on how to reduce air pollutant releases. The pollution sources are required to use the Maximum Available Control Technology (MACT)—a very high level of control—to reduce releases.

Sources which want to increase the amount of air toxics released, may choose to "offset" the increases so that their total hazardous air pollutant releases do not exceed their limitations. They may also choose to install pollution controls to keep pollutants at the required level.

A commonly used example of a toxic air pollutant is the woodburning stove. Woodburning stoves have become popular sources of inexpensive heat. Unfortunately, the smoke produced from the stove often contains particulates, such as soot and dust. The stoves also emit higher levels of hazardous air pollutants than smoke from oil or gas furnaces, and some of these pollutants have been linked to cancer. There has been an effort to redesign woodburning stoves so that they emit less pollution into the air. In that connection, the Clean Air Act has authorized the EPA to issue guidelines for the reduction of pollution from woodburning stoves.

Title IV: Acid Air Pollutants

Title IV of the Clean Air Act is concerned with acid air pollutants—commonly known as "acid rain." Acid air pollutants are harmful to our health and property, and damaging to the environment. The Clean Air Act has devised a program to reduce acid air pollutants.

The main source of acid rain are pollutants emitted from coalburning power plants. The coal contains sulfur which becomes sulfur dioxide (SO2)when the coal is burned. The larger the power plant, the more sulfur dioxide released into the air. These power plants also release nitrogen oxides (NOx). SO2 and NOx are chemicals related to sulfuric acid and nitric acid, two very strong acids.

These harmful pollutants are released into the air and carried by winds. If the wind blows the acid chemicals into areas of the country which experience wet weather, the acids actually become part of the precipitation, e.g., rain, snow or fog. If the wind blows the acid chemicals to dry areas of the country, they fall to the earth in dust or gas form.

When the acidic precipitation falls into waterways, such as lakes and streams, the water becomes very acidic. This in turn harms and destroys plant and animal life. Acid rain also makes the air hazy or foggy. Acid rain does more than environmental damage; it can damage health. Acid air pollution has been linked to severe respiratory problems.

To combat this problem, the Clean Air Act requires that annual releases of sulfur dioxide be reduced at least 40 percent, which should cause a major decrease in acid rain. In achieving this goal, the Clean Air Act has taken a market-based approach. Power plants may only release as much sulfur dioxide as they have "allowances" to do so. If a plant expects to release more sulfur dioxide than it has allowances, it has to obtain more allowances. They can buy or trade for more allowances from other power plants which have reduced their sulfur dioxide releases.

Every power plant is required to utilize continuous emissions monitoring systems which monitor the amount of SO2 and NOx being discharged. There are severe penalties for plants which release more pollutants than their allowances permit. Conversely, the law awards bonus allowances to power plants who assist in the effort to reduce sulfur dioxide, e.g. by using renewable energy, such as solar energy, or by installing cleaner coal technology.

Title V: Permit Program

Title V of the Clean Air Act established an operating permit program for larger sources of air pollution, e.g. power plants and factories. This permit program is modeled after the Federal National Pollution Elimination Discharge System (NPDES). The purpose of the permit program is to ensure compliance with the Clean Air Act, and to strengthen the EPA's enforcement capabilities. Businesses seeking permits have to pay permit fees which are used to pay for state air pollution control activities.

Requiring polluters to apply for a permit is not unique. Approximately 35 states have already implemented permit programs for air pollution. Under the EPA program, the permits are issued by the states. However, if a state fails to carry out the Clean Air Act provisions, the EPA can take over the permit issuance process.

The permit must include information on all types of pollutants being released; the quantity of each pollutant; and the source's pollution monitoring and reduction plan. Thus, the program ensures that all of a source's responsibilities relating to its pollutants will be contained in one permit document. This program assists the Federal and state agencies in its evaluation of the air quality situation.

Title VI: Stratospheric Ozone and Global Climate Protection

Title VI of the Clean Air Act is concerned with depletion of the ozone layer and global climate protection. Most people have heard about "holes" in the ozone layer. The ozone layer is a protective shield situated approximately 10 to 30 miles above the earth. It filters out harmful rays from the sun, such as the UV rays that have been linked with skin cancer. An ozone hole is not really a "hole" in this protective layer, but a thinning or worn area. Some ozone holes which have been discovered are as large as the United States.

Several decades ago, aerosol cans were linked with destruction of the ozone layer due to their use of propellants known as chlorofluorocarbons (CFCs) which were released into the air. As a result, the use of CFCs as propellants in aerosol cans was banned.

The Clean Air Act is concerned with repairing these ozone holes, however, this is a long-range task. A number of countries have already agreed to reduce production of chemicals that harm the ozone layer. However, there is no quick solution to repairing the ozone layer. The Clean Air Act sets forth a schedule for ceasing the production of ozone damaging chemicals.

Because a large number of consumer products contain ozone destroying chemicals and other harmful chemicals, they are subject to regulation under the Clean Air Act. Those products with the most damaging chemical make-up are required to label their product with a warning that the product: "contains or is manufactured with [the name of the chemical], a substance which harms public health and the environment by destroying ozone in the upper atmosphere." Products with a lesser damaging chemical make-up will have to be in compliance with the warning label by the year 2015.

Title VII: Enforcement

Title VII of the Clean Air Act is concerned with enforcement of its provisions. The Act contains a variety of authorities which make it more readily enforceable, as is the case with the other major environmental statutes.

The Act has empowered the EPA by strengthening their enforcement capabilities. The EPA has been given new authorities to issue administrative penalty orders of up to $200,000, and field citations up to $5000 for lesser infractions. The Act provides for greater civil judicial penalties, and the criminal penalties for willful violations have been upgraded from misdemeanors to felonies.

In addition, the Act allows private citizens the right to bring a citizen suit for penalties against a source, or the government, if the law is not enforced. The penalties go to a U.S. Treasury fund for use by EPA for compliance and enforcement activities.

CHAPTER 3:
INDOOR AIR QUALITY

IN GENERAL

Most people are aware of the damaging effects of outdoor air pollution on their health, however, they are not aware of the harmful health effects of indoor air pollution. According to the EPA, the indoor air levels of many pollutants may be 2-5 times, and occasionally more than 100 times, higher than outdoor levels. The EPA has ranked indoor air pollution among the top five environmental risks to public health.

This is significant because most people spend up to 90% of their time indoors. In addition, those most susceptible to the ill effects of indoor air pollutants spend the most time indoors, such as the elderly, the chronically ill and young children.

Human exposure to indoor air pollutants has increased over the last several decades for a number of reasons, including more tightly sealed construction, reduced ventilation to save energy, the use of synthetics in building materials and furnishings, and the use of chemicals in personal care products, pesticides, and household cleansers.

Although the indoor levels of one pollutant may not pose a significant health risk, it is the cumulative effect of the many potential sources of indoor air pollution that creates the most serious risk. There are steps that most people can take both to reduce the risk from existing sources and to prevent new problems from occurring.

To address this serious environmental problem, the EPA, working with other federal and state environmental agencies, has made a concerted effort to reduce this hazard in homes, schools and other buildings.

Directories of national and state information sources for indoor air quality are set forth at Appendix 6 and 7.

SOURCES OF INDOOR AIR POLLUTANTS

There are many sources of indoor air pollution which may include combustion sources such as oil, gas, kerosene, coal, wood, and tobacco products; building materials and furnishings such as asbestos-containing insulation, certain pressed wood products; household cleaning products; and personal care products; heating and cooling systems and humidification devices.

Whether a particular source is harmful depends in large part on the type and quantity of the pollutant it emits. If there is not enough outdoor air entering the home, the indoor air pollutants can accumulate to levels that may be harmful to one's health. Outdoor air enters and leaves a house by a number of methods: (i) infiltration, whereby outdoor air flows into the house through joints and cracks in walls, floors and ceilings; natural ventilation, whereby air enters through opened windows and doors; and mechanical ventilation., e.g., outdoor-vented fans. The rate at which outdoor air replaces indoor air is described as the air exchange rate. When there is little infiltration, natural ventilation, or mechanical ventilation, the air exchange rate is low and pollutant levels can increase.

According to the EPA, the most effective ways to improve indoor air quality are (i) to eliminate individual sources of pollution or to reduce their emissions; (ii) increase ventilation; or (iii) use an air cleaner to collect pollutants from the air. For most indoor air quality problems in the home, source control is the most effective solution.

The health effects of indoor air pollution may show up immediately after exposure or may not show up until many years after exposure. Immediate reactions may include eye, nose, and throat irritation, headache, dizziness, and fatigue. The symptoms of some diseases, such as asthma, may also show up soon after exposure. Health effects from long-term exposure may include respiratory diseases, heart disease, and cancer, and can be severely debilitating or fatal. Therefore, it is important to monitor indoor air quality even if there are no discernable symptoms.

COMMON INDOOR AIR POLLUTANTS

The most common indoor air pollutants include radon; environmental tobacco smoke (secondhand smoke); biological contaminants, such as pollen, mold and animal dander; combustion gases and particles emitted from devices such as woodburning stoves and furnaces; organic chemicals, such as those found in common household products; pesticides; asbestos; and lead.

A reference guide of major indoor air pollutants in the home is set forth at Appendix 8.

Radon

Radon is a colorless, odorless, radioactive gas which may be present indoors. The EPA recommends that people test their homes to find out whether radon is present in their home and, if so, at what level. The most common source of indoor radon is uranium in the soil or rock on which homes are built. As uranium naturally breaks down, it releases radon gas which can enter a home through dirt floors, and cracks in concrete walls and floors. When radon becomes trapped in buildings and concentrations build up indoors, exposure to radon becomes a health concern.

The predominant health effect associated with exposure to elevated levels of radon is lung cancer. Major health organizations agree that radon causes thousands of preventable lung cancer deaths each year. The EPA estimates that radon causes about 14,000 deaths per year in the United States—however, this number could range from 7,000 to 30,000 deaths per year. Further, if smoking takes place in the home, coupled with high radon levels, the risk of lung cancer is especially high.

Testing for radon is relatively simple using inexpensive, do-it-yourself radon test kits. The EPA recommends that consumers use test kits that are state-certified or have met the requirements of some national radon proficiency program.

A directory of state sources for radon information is set forth at Appendix 9.

Environmental Tobacco Smoke

Environmental tobacco smoke (ETS)—also known as "secondhand smoke"—is the mixture of smoke that comes from the burning end of a cigarette, pipe, or cigar, and the smoke exhaled by a smoker. It is a complex mixture of over 4,000 compounds, more than 40 of which are known to cause cancer in humans or animals and many of which are strong irritants.

According to the EPA, exposure to ETS is responsible for approximately 3,000 lung cancer deaths each year in nonsmoking adults and impairs the respiratory health of hundreds of thousands of children. It may also affect the cardiovascular system and some studies have linked exposure to secondhand smoke with the onset of chest pain.

Physical separation of smokers and nonsmokers indoors may reduce—but will not eliminate—the non-smokers' exposure to environmental tobacco smoke. The only way to eliminate the harmful effects of ETS is to prevent smoking indoors. If smoking indoors cannot be eliminated, it is important to increase ventilation.

Biological Contaminants

Biological contaminants include bacteria, molds, mildew, viruses, animal dander and cat saliva, house dust mites, cockroaches, and pollen. By controlling the relative humidity level in a home, the growth of some sources of biologicals can be minimized. A relative humidity of 30-50 percent is generally recommended for homes. Standing water, water-damaged materials, or wet surfaces also serve as a breeding ground for molds, mildews, bacteria, and insects. House dust mites, the source of one of the most powerful biological allergens, grow in damp, warm environments.

Some biological contaminants trigger allergic reactions, including hypersensitivity pneumonitis, allergic rhinitis, and some types of asthma. Infectious illnesses, such as influenza, measles, and chicken pox are transmitted through the air. Molds and mildews release disease-causing toxins. Symptoms of health problems caused by biological pollutants include sneezing, watery eyes, coughing, shortness of breath, dizziness, lethargy, fever, and digestive problems.

Exposure to biological contaminants can be reduced by using adequate ventilation methods and keeping humidity levels below 50 percent to prevent water condensation on building materials. If humidifiers are used in the home, they should be kept clean because they can become breeding grounds for biological contaminants

Combustion Gases and Particles

Unvented kerosene and gas space heaters, woodstoves, fireplaces, and gas stoves may release harmful combustion gases such as carbon monoxide, nitrogen dioxide, as well as particles. Combustion gases and particles also come from chimneys and flues that are improperly installed or maintained and cracked furnace heat exchangers.

Carbon monoxide is a colorless, odorless gas that interferes with the delivery of oxygen throughout the body. At high concentrations it can cause unconsciousness and death. Lower concentrations can cause a range of symptoms from headaches, dizziness, weakness, nausea, confusion, and disorientation, to fatigue in healthy people and episodes of increased chest pain in people with chronic heart disease.

Nitrogen dioxide is a colorless, odorless gas that irritates the mucous membranes in the eye, nose, and throat and causes shortness of breath after exposure to high concentrations. There is evidence that high concentrations or continued exposure to low levels of nitrogen dioxide increases the risk of respiratory infection and repeated exposure may lead, or contribute, to the development of lung disease such as emphysema.

Particles which are released when fuels are incompletely burned can lodge in the lungs and irritate or damage lung tissue. A number of carcinogenic pollutants, including radon, attach to small particles that are inhaled and are then carried deep into the lung.

It is important to follow manufacturers' instructions when using devices that may emit combustion gases. Proper ventilation is also important to reduce concentrations of such harmful emissions. In addition, chimneys and furnaces should be inspected annually and any necessary repairs should be made immediately.

Organic Chemicals

Organic chemicals are widely used as ingredients in household products, such as paints, varnishes, disinfectants, and cosmetics, and hobby products. Fuels are also made up of organic chemicals. All of these products can release harmful organic compounds which can persist at elevated concentration levels in the air following their use.

Some organic chemicals are highly toxic and others have no known deleterious health effects. Eye and respiratory tract irritation, headaches, dizziness, visual disorders, and memory impairment are among the immediate symptoms that some people have experienced soon after exposure to some organics. To reduce potential harmful effects, it is important to follow manufacturers' instructions, e.g., where a product warns that it should be used in a well-ventilated area.

Formaldehyde

Formaldehyde is an important chemical used to manufacture building materials, combustion devices, and numerous household products, and may be present in substantial concentrations both indoors and outdoors. Sources of formaldehyde in the home include building materials, smoking, household products, and the use of unvented, fuel-burning appliances, like gas stoves or kerosene space heaters.

In homes, the most significant sources of formaldehyde are likely to be pressed wood products such as particleboard shelving and furniture; hardwood plywood paneling; and medium density fiberboard used for cabinets and furniture tops.

Since 1985, the Department of Housing and Urban Development (HUD) has permitted only the use of plywood and particleboard that conform to specified formaldehyde emission limits in the construction of prefabricated and mobile homes. In the past, some of these homes had elevated levels of formaldehyde because of the large amount of high-emitting pressed wood products used in their construction.

Formaldehyde can cause watery eyes, burning sensations in the eyes and throat, nausea, and difficulty in breathing. It has also been shown to cause cancer in animals and may cause cancer in humans. To reduce the risk of formaldehyde exposure in the home, avoid the use of pressed wood products and other formaldehyde-emitting products.

Pesticides

According to the EPA, 75 percent of U.S. households used at least one pesticide product indoors during the past year. Pesticides used in and around the home include insecticides, termiticides, rodenticides, fungicides and disinfectants. Both the active and inert ingredients in pesticides can be organic compounds and thus have the same effects as other household products containing organic chemicals. Exposure to high levels of cyclodiene pesticides, commonly associated with misapplication, has produced various symptoms, including headaches, dizziness, muscle twitching, weakness, tingling sensations, and nausea. The EPA is also concerned that cyclodienes might cause long-term damage to the liver and the central nervous system, as well as an increased risk of cancer.

One should never use any pesticide that is designated for use by pest control specialists but should only use pesticides designated for use by the general public. The manufacturers' warnings should be carefully followed. Pesticides should be used in a well-ventilated area and, where possible, non-chemical pesticides should be substituted.

Asbestos

Asbestos is a mineral fiber that has been commonly used in a variety of building construction materials for insulation and as a fire-retardant. The EPA and Consumer Product Safety Commission have banned several asbestos products. Today, asbestos is most commonly found in older homes, e.g., in pipe and furnace insulation materials, asbestos shingles, and floor tiles.

Asbestos fibers can be very small and, if inhaled, they can accumulate in the lungs and cause such serious diseases as lung cancer, mesothelioma, and asbestosis. Symptoms of these diseases do not show up until many years after exposure began. Most people who develop asbestos-related diseases were exposed to elevated concentrations on the job and some developed disease from exposure to clothing and equipment brought home from work.

Elevated concentrations of airborne asbestos occur after asbestos-containing materials are disturbed by cutting, sanding or other remodeling activities. Improper attempts to remove these materials can release asbestos fibers into the air in homes, increasing asbestos levels and endangering people living in those homes. Thus, if asbestos is present in your home, it is usually best to leave any material that is in good condition alone because it will not likely release asbestos fiber. If the asbestos-containing material is damaged, one should contact their local health or environmental agency to find out about proper handling and disposal procedures.

Lead

Lead has been recognized as a harmful environmental pollutant which is particularly hazardous to the health of children. People are exposed to lead through air, drinking water, food, contaminated soil, deteriorating paint, and dust. Airborne lead enters the body when an individual breathes or swallows lead particles or dust once it has settled. Old lead-based paint is the most significant source of lead exposure and when improperly removed, e.g., by sanding, poses a harmful exposure.

Lead affects practically all systems within the body. High levels of exposure can cause convulsions, coma, and even death. Lower levels can adversely affect the brain, central nervous system, blood cells, and kidneys. The effects of lead poisoning in children have included serious developmental delays and brain damage.

CHAPTER 4:
WATER QUALITY

IN GENERAL

Prior to 1972, America's water resources were rapidly declining. The majority of the nation's waterways were unsafe for recreational activities, such as fishing and swimming. Soil was being eroded as a result of agricultural runoff, resulting in massive deposits of phosphorus and nitrogen into the waters. People were rightfully concerned about the safety of their drinking water.

THE CLEAN WATER ACT (33 U.S.C. 1251 ET SEQ.)

In response to public concern over the safety and cleanliness of our nation's water, Congress enacted The Clean Water Act in 1972. The Clean Water Act is the primary federal law protecting the integrity of our water. It is a comprehensive piece of legislation that has resulted in dramatic improvement in the quality of our water. The Act is carried out through the cooperative efforts of federal, state, local and tribal governments. The goals of the Clean Water Act are to eliminate the discharge of pollutants into our waterways, and achieve and maintain water quality levels that are suitable for recreational activities, such as fishing and swimming.

The Clean Water Act carries out its objectives by: (i) maintaining strict standards on water quality—e.g. it requires industry to meet certain performance standards to ensure water pollution control; (ii) offering financial aid to assist in compliance with the law—e.g., it authorizes funding to state and local governments to help them meet their clean water infrastructure needs; and (iii) protecting valuable wetlands and other aquatic habitats—e.g., it operates a permit process to ensure that land development is conducted in a manner that is beneficial to the environment.

The EPA works closely with other interested federal, state and local parties in an effort to maintain the integrity of the nation's water, including state ground water, drinking water, and Clean Water Act personnel; representatives of water systems; watershed managers; environmental and public health advocates; and agricultural interests groups. These parties are given the opportunity to participate directly in development of EPA guidance and policy.

In addition, the EPA has established partnerships with other Federal agencies; drinking water utilities; and non-profit organizations, to assist in the implementation of EPA standards. For example, in 1995, the Partnership for Safe Water was formed. The Partnership is a voluntary joint venture comprised of the EPA, states, and several national organizations representing drinking water systems.

The partnership developed a program to accelerate public health protection from the bacteria known as "cryptosporidium," as well as other microbial contaminants. This was accomplished by implementing a program to improve water filtration plant performance. Water utilities that complete phases of the program receive recognition from their peers and the EPA for these voluntary activities to pursue water quality goals beyond the regulations. Over 200 utilities that provide water to approximately 85 million persons are members of the Partnership.

Types of Regulated Pollutants

Pollutants regulated under the Clean Water Act fall under the categories of conventional pollutants, toxic pollutants, and nonconventional pollutants, as further set forth below.

Conventional Pollutants

Conventional pollutants are those contained in the wastewaters of homes, businesses and industries. Conventional pollutants are commonly found in human waste, laundry and bath water; and sink disposal deposits. They may include (i) fecal coliform—a bacteria found in human and animal digestive tracts that may indicate the potential presence of pathogenic organisms in water; and (ii) oil and grease—organic substances comprised of hydrocarbons, fats, oils, waxes, and/or high-molecular fatty acids, which may produce sludge solids that are difficult to process.

Toxic Pollutants

Toxic pollutants are categorized as either (i) organic—e.g., pesticides, solvents, polychlorinated biphenyls (PCBs), and dioxins; or (ii) metals—e.g., lead, silver, mercury, copper, chromium, zinc, nickel, and cadmium. Toxic pollutants are particularly harmful to plant and animal life.

Nonconventional Pollutants

Nonconventional pollutants are any substances that do not fall into the above two categories, but which require regulation, such as the nutrients nitrogen and phosphorus.

Major Provisions of Clean Water Act

The three major provisions of the Clean Water Act include: (i) the role of the National Pollutant Discharge Elimination System (NPDES) in protecting the nation's water, primarily through its permit program; (ii) The Oil Pollution Act, which sets forth the Federal government's authority relating to oil spills; and (iii) The Safe Drinking Water Act, which regulates and protects the integrity of the nation's drinking water.

The National Pollutant Discharge Elimination System

The NPDES Permit Program

The NPDES Permit Program is the mechanism by which the Clean Water Act ensures that there are no unauthorized discharges of pollutants into the nation's waters. The Act requires wastewater dischargers to obtain a permit. The permit establishes pollution limits, and specifies monitoring and reporting requirements. There are more than 200,000 sources regulated by NPDES permits nationwide.

The NPDES permits regulate household and industrial wastes that are collected in sewers and treated at municipal wastewater treatment plants. These permits also regulate industrial sources, and concentrated animal feeding operations, that discharge into other wastewater collection systems, or that discharge wastewater directly into receiving waters.

The goal of the NPDES permit program is to protect public health and aquatic life, and to make sure every facility treats their wastewater. The EPA uses a variety of methods to make sure permit holders comply with the conditions of their permits, such as conducting on-site inspections. If a regulated facility fails to comply with the provisions of its permit, it may be subject to enforcement actions.

The NPDES Watershed Program

The EPA's Office of Water Management (OWM) has developed the NPDES Watershed Strategy to ensure that watersheds are effectively protected. Under the Watershed Strategy, six areas have been identified that must be addressed to improve water quality: (i) Coordination with the states water protection programs; (ii) Streamlining the NPDES Permit Program; (iii) Developing state-wide monitoring strategy and requirements; (iv) Revising and updating existing national accountability measures; (v) Encouraging public participation in developing watershed protection plans and identifying local environmental goals; and (vi) Taking enforcement action against violators.

The NPDES Wet Weather Strategies

As set forth below, the NPDES is responsible for implementing wet weather strategies, such as (i) storm water management, and (ii) combined and sanitary sewer overflow control.

Storm Water Management

Storm water discharge from a number of sources is not easily controlled. Thus, the Clean Water Act has established a two-phased approach to remedying storm water discharges. Phase I of the program requires permits for separate storm water systems serving large and medium sized communities—i.e., those with over 100,000 inhabitants—and for storm water discharges associated with industrial and construction activity involving at least five acres.

Phase II of the program addresses remaining storm water discharges, such as those occurring in urban areas with populations under 100,000, smaller construction sites, and retail, commercial, and residential sites.

Combined and Sanitary Sewer Overflows

In 1994, the EPA issued a policy for the control of combined sewer overflows. Communities with combined sewer overflow problems are required to take immediate and long-term action to remedy the problem. This includes making sure that the sewer systems are operating properly, and receiving regular maintenance. In addition, a public notification requirement was included to ensure that the public receives prompt notification of the health and environmental impact of such overflows.

The EPA is currently in the process of evaluating the extent of sanitary sewer systems nationwide in an effort to identify any related issues which may pose a threat of harm to human health, property, and water quality.

The Oil Pollution Act (33 U.S.C. 2701 et seq.)

In 1990, Congress passed the Oil Pollution Act (OPA) in an effort to expand the prevention, preparedness, and response capabilities of the federal government and industry over oil discharges.

Oil spills pose serious threats to fresh water and marine environments. Oil spills adversely effect wildlife and their habitats. For example, the sad images of birds and mammals coated with oil and unable to function are often broadcast on the news following an oil spill.

In addition, the oil itself is toxic and poses a serious threat of harm, depending on the type of habitat. Some organisms may be seriously injured or killed very soon after contact with the oil, while other organisms suffer long-range effects, such as slow poisoning caused by long-term exposure to trapped oil.

Under Section 311(a)(1) of the Clean Water Act, "oil" is defined as "oil in any kind or in any form including, but not limited to, petroleum, fuel oil, sludge, oil refuse, and oil mixed with wastes other than dredged spoil." "Navigable waters" are broadly defined to include all waters that are used in interstate or foreign commerce, all interstate waters including wetlands, and all intrastate waters, such as lakes, rivers, streams, wetlands, sloughs, prairie potholes, wet meadows, playa lakes, or natural ponds.

The OPA amends Section 311 of the Clean Water Act, to (i) clarify federal response authority; (ii) increase penalties for oil spills; (iii) establish U.S. Coast Guard response organizations; (iv) require tank vessel and facility response plans; and (v) provide for contingency planning in designated areas.

The OPA also establishes a new liability and compensation system for oil spills into navigable waters; provides resources for the removal of discharged oil; and merges the funds established under several other laws in order to create a national spill trust fund.

The Safe Drinking Water Act

The Federal Safe Drinking Water Act (SDWA) was first enacted in 1974. In 1996, Congress passed amendments to the SDWA in order to strengthen the Act's public health protection by broadening its scope of action and level of public involvement. The SDWA amendments emphasize comprehensive public health protection through regulatory improvements, increased funding, prevention programs, and public participation. The existing law was improved in two important ways.

First, the amendments focus on setting risk-based priorities., i.e. a decision on which contaminants to regulate will be based on data concerning the adverse health effects of the contaminant, its occurrence in public water systems, and the projected risk reduction. Public health protection remains the primary concern on which drinking water standards are based.

Second, states have been given more flexibility to implement the Act to meet their specific needs. In addition, available funding has been increased through higher state drinking water program grants, and a new Drinking Water State Revolving Fund (DWSRF), designated for water system infrastructure improvements.

Providing safe water is a comprehensive and coordinated effort among the EPA, state, local and tribal governments, water suppliers, and the public. The amendments recognize that everyone has an interest in making sure the nation's drinking water is safe.

An important aspect of the amendments was the creation of the National Drinking Water Advisory Council (NDWAC). The NDWAC is a Federal advisory group whose role is to support the EPA's drinking water program by providing advice and recommendations to the EPA on drinking water issues. The NDWAC represents the drinking water community, including the public.

The SWDA amendments also established a microbial and disinfection byproducts advisory committee to assist the EPA in evaluating new data and information concerning microbial contaminants. Microbial contaminants, such as cryptosporidium and giardia, and byproducts of disinfection, have been identified as the highest potential drinking water risk to human health.

The SWDA amendments have made the reduction of this risk a priority, and require the EPA to set (i) new limits for disinfection byproducts in drinking water; (ii) removal requirements for cryptosporidium; and (iii) tighter standards for the cloudiness in suppliers' incoming water that may indicate microbial contamination.

In order to participate in the combined effort to maintain the integrity of our drinking water, individuals should familiarize themselves with the source of their drinking water, be aware of common indicators of contamination, and contact the appropriate authorities when a drinking water problem arises.

More than half of the nation's drinking water comes from underground wells. The rest of the drinking water comes from surface water sources, such as rivers, lakes and reservoirs. Tap water that meets the EPA and state standards is considered safe to drink. Thus, it is important to check whether the water supplier meets all of the required standards. The applicable state drinking water agency should be able to assist the consumer with this information.

Relevant provisions of The Safe Drinking Water Act are set forth at Appendix 10.

Testing Requirements

Under the SDWA, water systems that service in excess of 25 people are required to test their water regularly for a wide variety of contaminants. If the water system discovers that the presence of contaminants exceeds the EPA safety standard, they are required to take immediate action to correct the deficiency, and to alert the public about the problem and what action should be taken.

Individuals interested in having their own drinking water tested can call their state drinking water agency for a list of certified water testing labs. Each state is required to keep a list of all state-certified labs. The EPA does not test water quality for individuals.

Common Water Contaminants

Some of the more common water contaminants for which testing is required under the SWDA include:

Fecal Coliforms

Fecal coliforms are associated with sewage or animal waste. The presence of fecal coliforms in drinking water is usually caused by a problem with water treatment, or with the pipes that distribute the water. This may indicate that the water may be contaminated with organisms that can cause disease.

Lead

Lead is rarely in drinking water when it leaves the water treatment plant. Its presence in water usually comes from plumbing, particularly in older buildings that still have lead pipes. Children and pregnant women are most susceptible to health risks from lead in drinking water.

To reduce the amount of lead in drinking water, the EPA advises consumers to flush the cold water faucet by allowing the water to become cold before using it. One should never consume water from the hot water tap if lead is present. In addition, boiling only increases the concentration of lead in the water. You may be able to purchase a home water treatment unit that is designed to remove lead from the drinking water. Alternatively, use bottled water for drinking and cooking.

Copper

Blue-green water may be an indicator of high copper levels in the water. Adverse health effects of copper in the drinking water include stomach and intestinal distress, liver and kidney damage, and anemia. To reduce the amount of copper in drinking water, the EPA advises consumers to flush the cold water faucet by allowing the water to become cold before using it. One should never consume water from the hot water tap if copper is present. Hot water dissolves copper more quickly than cold water. You may be able to purchase a home water treatment unit that is designed to remove copper from the drinking water. Alternatively, use bottled water for drinking and cooking.

Radon

Radon is a soil gas that can affect underground sources of drinking water. If you are concerned about radon in your drinking water, you may have your water tested by a state-certified lab.

Cryptosporidium

Cryptosporidium is a parasite commonly found in lakes and rivers. It enters water supplies through sewage and animal waste. It causes cryptosporidiosis, a gastrointestinal disease. The most common symptom of cryptosporidiosis is watery, non-bloody diarrhea, often accompanied by abdominal cramps, nausea, vomiting, fever, headache, and/or loss of appetite. Generally, the disease is mild and people recover within one to three weeks. However, the disease can be severe, chronic, and even fatal for people with seriously weakened immune systems.

If there is concern that drinking water is contaminated, the EPA advises consumers to boil their water before using it. You may also be able to purchase a home water treatment unit that is designed to remove cryptosporidium from the drinking water. Alternatively, use bottled water for drinking and cooking.

CHAPTER 5:
HAZARDOUS MATERIALS AND SOLID WASTES

IN GENERAL

Years ago, the public was generally unaware of how dumping hazardous materials could affect their health and the health of the environment. The hazardous materials seeped into the ground, into rivers and lakes, and ultimately contaminated soil and groundwater. Many of these hazardous waste sites were subsequently abandoned, including landfills, warehouses, manufacturing facilities, and processing plants.

THE COMPREHENSIVE ENVIRONMENTAL RESPONSE, COMPENSATION AND LIABILITY ACT OF 1980 (42 U.S.C. 9601 ET SEQ.)

The public finally became aware of this serious health hazard. Their concern over the extent of the problem led Congress, in 1980, to enact The Comprehensive Environmental Response, Compensation and Liability Act (CERCLA) to eliminate the health and environmental threats posed by these hazardous waste sites. The U.S. Environmental Protection Agency (EPA) administers the Act through its Office of Solid Waste and Emergency Response (OSWER).

CERCLA—commonly referred to as "The Superfund Program"—is the most aggressive hazardous waste cleanup program in the world. The purpose of the Superfund Program is to provide authorities the ability to respond to uncontrolled releases of hazardous substances from inactive hazardous waste sites that endanger public health and the environment. It involves constant vigilance concerning situations that affect public health and the environment.

The Superfund Program uses the best available science to determine risks at sites, and to develop more expedient and less expensive ways to clean up the sites. If possible, old hazardous waste sites are restored to productive use. The Superfund Program authorizes the EPA to identify and clean up abandoned or uncontrolled hazardous waste sites, and to recover costs from parties responsible for the contamination. The Program also established prohibitions and requirements concerning closed and abandoned hazardous waste sites, and established a trust fund to provide for cleanup when no responsible party could be identified.

CERCLA further provided for the revision and republishing of the National Contingency Plan (40 CFR Part 300). The National Contingency Plan sets forth the guidelines and procedures needed to respond to releases and threatened releases of hazardous substances, pollutants, or contaminants, and provides for the National Priorities List, a list of hazardous waste sites in the country that are eligible for extensive, long-term cleanup under the Superfund program.

To evaluate the dangers posed by hazardous waste sites, EPA has developed a scoring system called the Hazard Ranking System. Sites that score high enough on the Hazard Ranking System are eligible for the National Priorities List. In addition, a site may be proposed for the National Priorities List if the Agency for Toxic Substances and Disease Registry issues a health advisory for the site, or if a state chooses a site for its top priority list.

Hazardous waste sites have been discovered by local and state agencies, businesses, the EPA, the U.S. Coast Guard, and by concerned citizens. The public can report suspected or potential hazardous waste sites to the National Response Center Hotline or to their state and local authorities.

Emergency Response

Some situations involving hazardous waste are emergencies—such as those involving toxic chemicals—and require immediate action. Emergency actions are designed to eliminate immediate risks to public health and safety. Typical chemical emergencies may include train derailments, truck accidents, and incidents at chemical plants where there is a chemical release or threat of a release to the environment. Superfund's number one priority is to protect the people in communities near sites and their environment. The hazardous materials are removed from the site for treatment or proper disposal, or they are treated at the site to make them safe. The EPA then evaluates the site and determines whether additional cleanup is necessary.

Non-Emergency Situations

When a potential hazardous waste site is reported, the EPA investigates the site to determine what type of action is necessary. The EPA may interview local residents to find out more about the site's history, and whether it has caused any adverse effects on the population or the environment.

Some sites do not require any action, while others are referred to the state, or other agencies, for cleanup or further action. For sites which require EPA intervention, it tests the soil, water, and air to determine what hazardous substances were left at the site and how serious the risks may be to human health and the environment. The EPA uses the information collected to decide what type of action, if any, is required. Parties responsible for the contamination at the site are also permitted to conduct these assessments under close EPA supervision.

The EPA then prepares a Community Relations Plan based on discussions with local leaders and private citizens in the community, and sets up a local information file in the community so that the public can access information about the site. The file contains the official record of the site—known as the Administrative Record—as well as additional site-related information.

Early Action

Early action is taken when the EPA determines that a site may soon become a threat to the public or the environment. For example, there may be a site where leaking drums of hazardous substances could catch on fire. Typical early action is taken to:

1. Prevent direct human contact with contaminants from the site;

2. Remove hazardous materials from the site;

3. Prevent contaminants from spreading off the site;

4. Provide water to residents whose drinking water has been contaminated by the site; or

5. Temporarily or permanently evacuate or relocate local residents.

Long-Term Cleanups

Early action can correct many hazardous waste problems and eliminate most threats to human health and the environment. Some sites, however, require long-term action. These sites were caused by years of pollution and may take several years, or even decades, to clean up.

Long-term cleanups are extensive and involve a number of steps. First, a detailed study of the site is done to identify the cause and extent of contamination at the site, the possible threats to public health and the environment, and ways to clean up the site. The EPA then develops what is called a Proposed Plan for Long-Term Cleanup, which is made available to the public, and to local and state officials for comment.

Once all concerns are addressed, the EPA publishes a Record of Decision, which describes their plan to clean up the site. The subsequent design and actual cleanup of the site is conducted by EPA, the state, or by the parties responsible for the contamination.

The EPA regularly monitors every National Priorities List site to make sure it remains safe. If there is any indication that a problem has arisen, immediate action is taken to make the site safe again.

Superfund Participants

Superfund cleanups are very complex and require the efforts of many experts in science, engineering, public health, management, law, community relations, and numerous other fields. The goal of the process is to protect the public, and the environment, from the effects of hazardous substances. Community involvement is very important. The public has the opportunity and the right to be involved in—and to comment on—the cleanup work being undertaken.

The Technical Assistance Grant Program

The EPA values public input. It endeavors to assist concerned citizens in understanding the technical information relating to the cleanup of Superfund sites in their community, so that informed decisions can be made.

Under the Superfund law, the EPA can award communities grants, known as Technical Assistance Grants, of up to $50,000 per site. Technical Assistance Grants allow communities to hire an independent expert to help them interpret technical data, understand site hazards, and become more knowledgeable about the different technologies that are being used to cleanup sites. More information about Technical Assistance Grants is available from a Regional EPA Community Involvement Coordinator.

Community Advisory Group Program

One of the ways communities can participate in site cleanup decisions is by forming a Community Advisory Group. A Community Advisory Group is made up of representatives of diverse community interests. Its purpose is to provide a public forum for community members to present and discuss their concerns related to the Superfund decision-making process. Contact a Regional EPA Community Involvement Coordinator for more information about the Community Advisory Group Program.

Costs

Under the Superfund law, the EPA is able to make those companies and individuals responsible for contamination at a Superfund site perform, and pay for, the cleanup work at the site. The EPA negotiates with the responsible parties to get them to pay for the plans and the work that has to be done to clean up the site. If an agreement cannot be reached, the EPA issues orders to responsible parties to make them clean up the site under EPA supervision.

The EPA may also use Superfund Trust Fund money to pay for cleanup costs, and then attempt to get the money back through legal action. The Superfund Trust Fund was set up to pay for the cleanup of these sites. The money comes mainly from taxes on the chemical and petroleum industries. The Trust Fund is used primarily when those companies or people responsible for contamination at Superfund sites cannot be found, or cannot perform or pay for the cleanup work.

THE RESOURCE CONSERVATION AND RECOVERY ACT (42 U.S.C. 6901 ET SEQ.)

In 1976, to address the dangers hazardous wastes pose, Congress enacted the Resource Conservation and Recovery Act (RCRA). The Act established a national program to ensure that hazardous wastes are managed safely from the point of generation to final disposal ("cradle to grave"). The RCRA regulates the identification, transportation, treatment, storage, and disposal of solid and hazardous wastes. In implementing the Act, the EPA has created a complex regulatory framework addressing solid waste disposal and hazardous waste management.

The RCRA regulates such items as: (i) hazardous waste generators and transporters; (ii) land disposal restrictions; (iii) federal procurement of products that contain recycled materials; (iv) municipal solid waste landfill criteria; (v) solid and hazardous waste recycling; (vi) treatment, storage and disposal facilities; and (viii) waste minimization and hazardous waste combustion.

Although the RCRA mostly deals with hazardous waste, Congress also made provisions in the Act for state and regional solid waste management plans. As the space in landfills is used up, solid waste management has become an important environmental concern. Recycling and elimination of many of the sources of such waste needs to be undertaken in order to reduce the volume of solid waste production.

Some states have found ways to use solid wastes to their benefit. For example, incineration systems—known as resource recovery facilities—generate electricity by using heat from burning solid waste to produce steam. However, these facilities have raised other concerns, e.g. dioxin emissions.

THE OFFICE OF UNDERGROUND STORAGE TANKS (OUST)

An underground storage tank (UST) system is a tank (or a combination of tanks) and connected piping having at least 10 percent of their combined volume underground. The tank system includes the tank, underground connected piping, underground ancillary equipment, and any containment system.

In 1984, due to concern over the harmful effects of releases—e.g., leaks and spills—from underground storage tanks, Congress directed the EPA to develop regulations for underground storage tank systems. The EPA's Office of Underground Storage Tanks (OUST) developed the Federal regulations which delegate UST regulatory authority to approved State programs. States with approved programs operate in lieu of the Federal regulations.

A directory of internet addresses for state underground storage tank programs is set forth at Appendix 11.

Federally Regulated Underground Storage Tanks

Federally regulated USTs meet one or more of the following criteria:

1. The UST has a capacity of more than 110 gallons;

2. The UST contains regulated substances as defined as hazardous under the CERCLA, with certain exceptions;

3. The UST does not contain hazardous wastes regulated—i.e., listed or identified—under Subtitle C of the Solid Waste Disposal Act, or a mixture of such hazardous waste and another regulated substance; and/or

4. The UST is not part of a wastewater treatment system that is part of a wastewater treatment facility regulated under section 402 or 307(b) of the Clean Water Act.

Under the Code of Federal Regulations (40 CFR part 280.11), the following types of tanks do not have to meet federal UST regulations:

1. Farm and residential tanks of 1,100 gallons or less capacity holding motor fuel used for noncommercial purposes;

2. Tanks storing heating oil used on the premises where it is stored;

3. Tanks on or above the floor of underground areas, such as basements or tunnels;

4. Septic tanks and systems for collecting storm water and wastewater;

5. Flow-through process tanks;

6. Tanks of 110 gallons or less capacity; and

7. Emergency spill and overfill tanks.

Some state and/or local regulatory authorities, however, may include these tank types in their UST regulations so the reader is advised to check with their state and local authorities if you have questions about the requirements for a particular type of tank.

Applicability of some of the Federal UST regulations has been deferred for the following systems, however, releases from these systems must still undergo corrective action:

1. Wastewater treatment tank systems;

2. Any UST systems containing radioactive materials that are regulated under the Atomic Energy Act of 1954 (42 U.S.C.2011);

3. Any UST system that is part of an emergency generator system at nuclear power generation facilities regulated by the Nuclear Regulator Commission under 10 C.F.R. Part 50, Appendix A;

4. Airport hydrant fuel distribution systems; and

5. UST systems with field-constructed tanks.

USTs storing fuel solely for use by emergency power generators are deferred from only the release detection requirements.

UST Releases

According to the EPA, more than 300,000 releases have been reported from Underground Storage Tank (UST) systems. These releases have been caused by leaks, spills and overfills from UST systems. Many have posed serious threats to human health and the environment. In particular, petroleum products contain many potentially hazardous and toxic chemicals. Fumes and vapors can travel beneath the ground and collect in areas such as basements, utility vaults, and parking garages where they can pose a serious threat of explosion, fire, and suffocation or other adverse health effects.

Gasoline, leaking from service stations, is a common source of groundwater pollution. Because approximately one-half of the population of the United States relies on groundwater as their source of drinking water, groundwater pollution is a serious problem. Many municipal and private wells have had to be shut down as the result of contamination caused by releases from UST systems.

The mission of the UST program is to protect human health and environmental quality by requiring proper management of underground storage tank systems. Good tank management includes prevention, detection, and timely, cost-effective cleanup of releases. The two primary goals of the UST Program are prevention and cleanup, as set forth below:

Prevention

The EPA endeavors to prevent the creation of a new generation of leaking USTs. Reaching this goal requires that USTs be protected from corrosion, protected against spills and overfills, equipped to detect releases, and be properly installed and maintained.

Cleanup

The EPA works to ensure that UST releases are detected and cleaned up promptly and cost-effectively to the extent necessary to protect human health and the environment. Regular monitoring of UST systems by owners and operators ensure that releases are promptly detected.

Detecting UST Releases

Releases from UST systems can originate from one or more of the system components, as well as from spills and overfills. Because most of the components are buried underneath the ground, the owner/operator must rely on methods other than sight and smell to determine if a release has occurred, including recognition of the following warning signals:

1. Unusual operating conditions, such as erratic behavior of the dispensing pump.

2. Results from leak detection monitoring and testing that indicate a leak.

3. Reports from fuel delivery drivers; or

4. Complaints from neighbors about vapors in their basements or about water that tastes or smells like petroleum.

Any suspected release must be reported immediately to the state or local implementing agency. Quick action can minimize the extent of environmental damage, and the threat to human health and safety, and the responsible party's share of the cleanup cost.

THE OFFICE OF SITE REMEDIATION ENFORCEMENT

The Office of Site Remediation Enforcement (OSRE) strives to protect human health and the quality of the environment by providing direction, evaluation, oversight and assistance for remediation enforcement at non-federally owned sites subject to the RCRA, CERCLA, the Oil Pollution Act (OPA), and the UST Program. The OSRE provides the means for states to vigorously and effectively enforce these statutes. The OSRE's goal is to achieve prompt site cleanup and maximum liable party participation in performing and paying for cleanup in ways which promote environmental justice and fairness.

THE OFFICE OF SOLID WASTE AND EMERGENCY RESPONSE

The Office of Solid Waste and Emergency Response (OSWER) provides agency-wide policy, guidance and direction for the EPA's solid waste and emergency response programs. The Office develops guidelines and standards for the land disposal of hazardous wastes and for underground storage tanks. The Office furnishes technical assistance in the development, management and operation of solid waste activities and analyzes the recovery of useful energy from solid waste.

The Office has also undertaken the development and implementation of a program to respond to abandoned and active hazardous waste sites and accidental releases, including some oil spills, as well as the encouragement of innovative technologies for contaminated soil and groundwater.

OSWER is comprised of the following offices:

1. Chemical Emergency Preparedness & Prevention;

2. Federal Facilities Restoration and Reuse;

3. Hazardous Waste Technology Innovations;

4. Oil Spill Program;

5. Office of Solid Waste: Hazardous, Non-Hazardous & Special; and

6. A Special Initiatives Office

THE FEDERAL INSECTICIDE, FUNGICIDE AND RODENTICIDE ACT (7 U.S.C. 136 ET SEQ.)

Under the Federal Insecticide, Fungicide and Rodenticide Act (FIRFA), the EPA is charged with regulating the manufacture and packaging of pesticides. The use of pesticides is strictly controlled, and public notice is generally required when pesticides have been applied in public areas, such as restaurants. Further, the EPA requires that all pesticides be registered, and labeled and packaged according to the requirements set forth in the Act.

THE EMERGENCY PLANNING AND COMMUNITY RIGHT-TO-KNOW ACT (42 U.S.C. 11001 ET. SEQ.)

In November of 1986, Congress enacted The Emergency Planning and Community Right-to-Know Act (EPCRA), in large part due to the extreme danger posed by the bulk storage of petroleum and hazardous substances, even in small quantities. In passing this law, Congress recognized the need for local and state officials to be aware of such potential hazards.

The EPCRA was also designed to help communities prepare for chemical emergencies that may result from leakages. It allows the public, and local and state governmental officials, access to information about potential chemical hazards, such as the location and volume of all storage sites. The EPCRA established emergency planning and reporting requirements for facilities that store hazardous chemicals.

Common EPCRA topics include: emergency planning; hazardous chemical inventory reporting; public access to chemical information; toxic chemical release reporting; and the toxic release inventory (TRI) database. Hotline EPCRA specialists also answer questions on the accidental release prevention provisions of the Clean Air Act.

CHAPTER 6:
BIODIVERSITY CONSERVATION

IN GENERAL

Human life depends on biological diversity. Marine ecosystems and the diversity of species that inhabit the ecosystems provide us with such necessities as food, medicine, and clean air to breathe. However, human actions are threatening the natural development of these ecosystems and disturbing the marine species and their habitats. A number of federal agencies, including the U.S. Fish and Wildlife Service, The National Marine Fisheries Service, the Environmental Protection Agency, along with state and local environmental agencies, work together to coordinate programs, such as the National Estuaries Program, that study, conserve, and manage biological diversity. These agencies also implement and enforce legislation, such as the Clean Water Act and the Endangered Species Act, designed to protect, conserve and restore marine resource habitat and biodiversity.

WETLANDS

Wetlands are generally defined as areas where the recurrent and extended presence of water at or near the soil surface is responsible for the kind of soils that form, and the plant and animal life that inhabit the area. The lower 48 states contained an estimated 103.3 million acres of wet lands in the mid-1980s. An estimated 170-200 million acres of wetland exist in Alaska. Hawaii has 52,000 acres of wetland.

Recent estimates of wetlands trends on non-federal lands indicate a loss rate between 70,000 to 90,000 acres annually. This is due to both natural threats, such as erosion and droughts, and human actions, such as draining, dredging, construction and mining.

In addition to these losses, many other wetlands have suffered degradation of functions. These losses, as well as degradation, have greatly diminished our nation's wetlands resources. As a result, we no longer have the benefits they provided. The increase in flood damages, drought damages, and the declining bird populations are, in part, the result of wetlands degradation and destruction. All of these impacts could affect species composition and wetland functions. Due to concern over the loss of wetlands and the resulting negative effects on the environment, federal and state legislation has been enacted to protect the wetlands.

The federal government protects wetlands through regulations such as Section 404 of the Clean Water Act, economic incentives and disincentives, cooperative programs, and acquisition—e.g., establishing national wildlife refuges.

Beyond the federal level, a number of states have enacted laws to regulate activities in wetlands, and some counties and towns have adopted local wetlands protection ordinances or have changed the way development is permitted.

Most coastal states have significantly reduced losses of coastal wetlands through such protective laws. Few states, however, have laws specifically regulating activities in inland wetlands, although some states and local governments have non-regulatory programs that help protect wetlands.

Importance of Wetlands

There is growing recognition of the important contributions wetlands make to our environment. Wetlands are so ecologically beneficial, that they have been compared to the tropical rain forests and coral reefs. Wetlands improve water quality by filtering runoff and adjacent surface waters—removing or retaining its nutrients, processing organic wastes, and reducing sediment before it reaches open water—thus protecting our lakes, bays and rivers, as well as many of our drinking water sources. Wetlands function like natural sponges, storing water and slowly releasing it, helping to slow floodwaters and reduce erosion at the shorelines.

In addition, rare and beautiful species of plant and animal life have been found to inhabit wetland areas, as well as many commercially and recreationally valuable species of fish and wildlife. The U.S. Fish and Wildlife Service estimates that a large number of the threatened and endangered species rely directly or indirectly on wetlands for their survival. Wetlands are also a great source of natural products, including fish, timber, wild rice, and furs.

Identifying Wetlands

Generally, wetlands are lands where saturation with water is the dominant factor determining the nature of soil development in the area, and the types of plant and animal life inhabiting the area. Wetlands vary widely because of regional and local differences in such factors as climate, type of soil, topography, and vegetation, etc., and are found on every continent except Antarctica.

The term "wetlands" is the collective word used to refer to marshes, swamps, bogs, and similar areas found in flat vegetated areas; in depressions in the landscape; and between dry land and water along the edges of streams, rivers, lakes, and coastlines. Many "wetlands" only contain water for a short period of time. The rest of the time they appear to be dry land, making it difficult sometimes to identify a wetland area.

One method used to identify wetlands is to observe them in the growing season, when the upper part of the soil is saturated with water. It is at this time that soil organisms consume the oxygen in the soil and cause conditions unsuitable for most plants. These conditions cause the development of "hydric soils" which are different in color and texture. Plants that are able to grow in such conditions are called "hydrophytes." The appearance of hydric soils and hydrophytes indicates the presence of wetlands.

Common examples of wetlands include swamps, bogs and marshes. Less recognized examples include (i) vernal pools—pools that form in the spring rains but are dry at other times of the year; (ii) playas—areas at the bottom of undrained desert basins that are sometimes covered with water; and (iii) prairie potholes. A description of some of the important types of wetlands are set forth below.

Bogs

A bog is characterized by spongy peat deposits, a growth of evergreen trees and shrubs, and a floor covered by a thick carpet of sphagnum moss. The only water source for bogs is rainwater. Bogs have extremely low nutrient levels that form acidic peat deposits. Much of the acidity in bogs is due to sulfuric acid formed by the oxidation of organic sulfur compounds and from humic acids produced in the water. Bogs serve important ecological functions in preventing downstream flooding by absorbing direct precipitation and runoff, protecting water quality by intercepting and filtering runoff, and providing critical habitat for unique plant and animal life able to survive on the low-nutrient diet. Bogs are found in the northern hemisphere.

Bottomland Hardwoods

Bottomland hardwood forests are river swamps, found along rivers and streams generally in the broad floodplain of the southeast and south central United States. They are deciduous forested wetlands, made up of different species of gum and oak, which have the ability to survive in areas that are either seasonally flooded or covered with water much of the year. Bottomland Hardwoods serve a critical role in the watershed by reducing the risk and severity of flooding to downstream communities. In addition, these wetlands improve water quality by filtering and flushing nutrients, processing organic wastes, and reducing sediment before it reaches open water.

Fens

Fens are a type of open freshwater marsh. Fens receive nutrients from sources other than precipitation, e.g. upslope sources through drainage from surrounding mineral soils and groundwater movement. Unlike bogs, peats associated with fens are not acidic and have higher nutrient mineral levels, and are therefore able to support much more diverse plant and animal life. Like bogs, fens are found in the northern hemisphere. Fens also provide important benefits to a watershed, including preventing or reducing the risk of floods, improving water quality, and providing habitat for unique plant and animal life.

Prairie Potholes

Prairie potholes are depressional wetlands found primarily in the Upper Midwest. They are generally comprised of freshwater marshes. Some prairie pothole marshes are temporary, while others may be permanent. This region, because of the numerous shallow lakes and marshes, the rich soils, and the warm summers, is described as being one of the most important wetland regions in the world. The area is home to more than 50 percent of North American migratory waterfowl, with many species dependent on the potholes for breeding and feeding. Prairie potholes serve to reduce the risk and severity of downstream flooding by absorbing rain, snow melt, and floodwaters and slowly releasing it.

Vernal Pools

Vernal pools are naturally occurring depressional wetlands that are covered by shallow water for variable periods from winter to spring, but may be completely dry for most of the summer and fall. These wetlands range in size from small puddles to shallow lakes and are usually found in a gently sloping plain of grassland. Beneath vernal pools lies either bedrock or a hard clay layer that helps keep water in the pool. The unique environment of vernal pools provides habitat for numerous rare plants and animals that are able to survive the harsh conditions. Many of these plants and animals spend the dry season as seeds, eggs, or cysts, and then grow and reproduce when the ponds are flooded again.

In addition, birds such as egrets, ducks, and hawks use vernal pools as a seasonal source of food and water.

The U.S. Environmental Protection Agency—Wetlands Division

The stated mission of the EPA's Wetlands Division is to encourage and enable others to act effectively in protecting and restoring the nation's wetlands and associated ecosystems, including shallow open waters and free-flowing streams.

A Directory of Regional EPA Wetlands Division Offices is set forth at Appendix 12.

In carrying out its mission, the Wetlands Division is primarily responsible for (i) establishing national standards; and (ii) assisting others to comply with those standards.

In order to most effectively restore and maintain the nation's wetlands, the EPA's Wetlands Division incorporates an integrated wetlands/watershed approach in much of its work with other interested agencies. A watershed—also called a drainage basin—is the area in which all water, sediments, and dissolved materials flow or drain from the land into a common river, lake, ocean, or other body of water. The wetlands are considered important elements of a watershed because they serve as the link between land and water resources.

An integrated watershed-based approach to water and wetlands protection considers the whole system, including other resource management programs that address land, air, and water, to successfully manage problems for a given aquatic resource. The integrated approach recognizes that the quality of the nation's wetlands and other water resources is directly linked to the quality of the environment surrounding these waters.

Wetland Regulation Under the Clean Water Act

For regulatory purposes under the Clean Water Act, the EPA and the U.S. Army Corps of Engineers have defined wetlands as "those areas that are inundated or saturated by surface or ground water at a frequency and duration sufficient to support, and that under normal circumstances do support, a prevalence of vegetation typically adapted for life in saturated soil conditions."

In protecting the wetlands, the EPA and the Corps of Engineers jointly (i) administer the Section 404 Permit Program pursuant to the Clean Water Act; and (ii) take enforcement action against violators.

The Section 404 Permit Program

Section 404 of the Clean Water Act establishes a program to regulate the discharge of dredged and fill material into waters of the United States, including wetlands. The program's objective is to prevent any discharge of dredged or fill material into wetlands or waters, if a practicable alternative exists that is less damaging to the aquatic environment, or if the discharge would cause a significant adverse effect on the nation's waters.

Regulated activities are controlled by a permit review process. An individual permit is usually required for potentially significant impacts. However, for most discharges that will have only minimal adverse effects, up-front general permits are often granted. Section 404(f) exempts some activities from regulation, including many ongoing farming, ranching, and silviculture practices.

The EPA and the Army Corps of Engineers jointly administer the Section 404 permit program. Other agencies, including the U.S. Fish and Wildlife Service, the National Marine Fisheries Service, and various state resource agencies have important advisory roles in the process.

If an individual permit is required, public notice must be issued by the Corps of Engineers within 15 days of receiving all permit information. The public notice describes the permit application, including the proposed activity, its location, and potential environmental impacts. The public notice also invites comments which must be submitted within a specified period of time. The application and comments are then reviewed by the Corps of Engineers and other interested Federal and State agencies, organizations, and individuals. The Corps determines whether an Environmental Impact Statement (EIS) is necessary. An EIS is a report which sets forth the proposed action; its impact on the environment and energy sources; available alternatives; and mitigation measures. The EIS is generally made available to the public for review and comment before a permit can be issued.

The Corps of Engineers evaluates the permit application based on the comments received, as well as its own evaluation. The permit decision is set forth in a document known as a Statement of Finding, which is also made available to the public.

Section 404 Enforcement

In addition to jointly implementing the Section 404 permit program, the EPA and the Corps of Engineers share Section 404 enforcement authority. Violations under Section 404 generally include (i) the failure to comply with the terms or conditions of a Section 404 permit; or (ii) the discharge of dredged or fill material to waters of the United States without a permit. Violators are subject to a wide variety of enforcement actions.

Administrative Enforcement

The EPA can issue administrative compliance orders requiring the violator to stop any ongoing illegal discharge activity and to remove the illegal discharge and restore the site. The EPA and the Corps can also assess administrative civil penalties of up to $125,000 per illegal action.

Judicial Enforcement

The EPA and the Corps of Engineers have the authority to take civil judicial action, seeking restoration and other types of injunctive relief, as well as civil penalties.

Criminal Enforcement

The EPA and the Corps of Engineers also have authority to bring criminal judicial enforcement actions for knowingly or negligently violating Section 404.

CORAL REEFS

Coral reefs represent one of the most diverse ecosystems in the world and are often referred to as "the rainforests of the ocean." Corals are tiny sessile animals which are not mobile but stay fixed in one place. They feed by reaching out with tentacles to catch prey such as small fish and planktonic animals. Corals live in colonies consisting of many individuals. They secrete a hard calcium carbonate skeleton. It is these hard skeletal structures that build up coral reefs over time. Reef building corals are found in shallow, clear water in tropical or sub-tropical temperatures. Coral reefs provide habitats for a large variety of organisms. These organisms rely on corals as a source of food and shelter.

Coral reefs are sensitive indicators of water quality and the ecological integrity of the ecosystem. They are important fishery and nursery areas and provide protection from erosion to coastlines and sand for beaches. However, as with wetlands, coral reefs are suffering natural and human-induced stresses. The federal government has recognized the need to help protect these natural resources.

On June 11, 1998 President Clinton issued Executive Order 13089 on Coral Reef Protection "to preserve and protect the biodiversity, health, heritage, and social and economic value of U.S. coral reef ecosystems and the marine environment." The presidential directive was issued as part of the National Ocean Conference, a meeting of U.S. ocean policy makers convened to mark the International Year of the Ocean.

The Executive Order directs all federal agencies to protect coral reef ecosystems to the extent feasible, and established the U.S. Coral Reef Task Force. Task Force duties include coral reef mapping and monitoring; research aimed at identifying the major causes and consequences of degradation of coral reef ecosystems; and implementation of conservation, mitigation, and restoration measures.

ESTUARIES

An estuary is a partially enclosed body of water formed where freshwater from rivers and streams flows into the ocean, mixing with the salty sea water. Estuaries and the lands surrounding them are places of transition from land to sea, and from fresh to salt water.

The tidal, sheltered waters of estuaries support unique communities of plants and animals, specially adapted for life at the margin of the sea. Estuarine environments are among the most productive on earth, creating more organic matter each year than comparably-sized areas of forest, grassland, or agricultural land. The productivity and variety of estuarine habitats host a diversity of wildlife.

Estuaries are critical for the survival of many species. In addition, the wetlands that fringe many estuaries also perform other valuable services. For example, water draining from the uplands carry sediments, nutrients, and other pollutants. As the water flows through fresh and salt marshes, much of the sediments and pollutants are filtered out. This filtration process creates cleaner and clearer water, which benefits both people and marine life. Estuarine plants also help prevent erosion and stabilize the shoreline.

It has been recognized that estuaries are an irreplaceable natural resource that must be managed carefully for the mutual benefit of all who enjoy and depend on them. The National Estuary Program was established in 1987 by amendments to the Clean Water Act to identify, restore, and protect nationally significant estuaries of the United States.

The Environmental Protection Agency (EPA) administers the National Estuary Program, but program decisions and activities are carried out by committees of local government officials, private citizens, and representatives from other federal agencies, academic institutions, industry, and estuary user-groups.

EFFECTS OF ACID RAIN

As set forth in Chapter 2, acid rain is caused by the emission of sulfur dioxide and nitrogen oxide from coalburning plants. These highly acidic pollutants are released into the air. If the wind blows the acid chemicals into areas of the country which experience wet weather, the acids actually become part of the precipitation, e.g., rain, snow or fog.

The ecological effects of acid rain are demonstrated in the aquatic environments, such as streams, lakes, and marshes, etc. Acid rain flows to streams, lakes, and marshes after falling on forests, fields, buildings, and roads. Acid rain also falls directly on aquatic habitats and causes a number of effects that harm or kill individual fish, reduce fish population numbers, completely eliminate fish species from a waterbody, and decrease biodiversity. As acid rain flows through soils in a watershed, aluminum is released from soils into the lakes and streams located in that watershed. As the pH level in a lake or stream decreases, the aluminum level increases. Low pH and increased aluminum levels are directly toxic to fish and other aquatic organisms.

The plants and animals living within an ecosystem are interdependent. Some types of plants and animals are able to tolerate acidic waters. Others, however, are acid-sensitive and will be lost as the pH declines. Some acid lakes have no fish. For example, frogs appear to be able to better tolerate acidic water. However if the food source that the frogs depend upon cannot tolerate acidity, the food source will disappear and necessarily affect the frogs.

Because of these connections among the many fish, plants, and other organisms living in an aquatic ecosystem, changes in pH or aluminum levels affect biodiversity as well. Thus, as lakes and streams become more acidic, the numbers and types of fish and other aquatic plants and animals that live in these waters decrease.

Under Title IV of the Clean Air Act, a program to reduce acid air pollutants has been devised. As set forth in Chapter 2, it requires plants to continuously monitor its emissions and restricts the amount of pollutants that a plant can emit. It also assesses penalties to plants which exceed their allowed emissions and offers incentives to plants which assist in finding ways to reduce toxic emissions.

CHAPTER 7:
ENDANGERED SPECIES

IN GENERAL

Species and habitat endangerment and extinction is one of the most urgent environmental problems facing society today. Habitat extinction is a critical part of the problem because species cannot live without their supporting environment. Thus, habitat extinction is causally connected to animal extinction. In fact, the leading cause of species endangerment and extinction is loss of habitat, which is primarily caused by mankind.

Another major cause of species endangerment and extinction involves the accidental or intentional introduction of a species into a new setting, thereby disrupting the delicate ecological balance of the existing habitat.

The third leading cause of species endangerment and extinction is overexploitation. Overexploitation refers to the use of a particular species at a rate that leads to endangerment or extinction of that species.

For example, according to the African Wildlife Foundation, the volume of world trade in ivory from 1980 to 1985 was 800 tons per year. In order to meet such a demand, approximately 90,000 elephants had to be killed yearly. This caused a depletion in the African elephant population. In 1979, there were approximately 1,300,000 African elephants in existence, whereas there are presently less than 650,000.

Although species extinction is historically a natural occurrence, it has increased at an unprecedented rate primarily due to human activity which does not allow for species adaptation. As a result, it is estimated that hundreds of thousands of species may become extinct in the near future.

MARINE MAMMAL PROTECTION ACT

Findings and Purpose

The Marine Mammal Protection Act of 1972 (MMPA) was most recently reauthorized in 1994. In passing the MMPA in 1972, Congress found that:

1. Certain species and population stocks of marine mammals are, or may be, in danger of extinction or depletion as a result of man's activities;

2. Such species and population stocks should not be permitted to diminish beyond the point at which they cease to be a significant functioning element in the ecosystem of which they are a part, and, consistent with this major objective, they should not be permitted to diminish below their optimum sustainable population level;

3. Measures should be taken immediately to replenish any species or population stock which has diminished below its optimum sustainable level;

4. There is inadequate knowledge of the ecology and population dynamics of such marine mammals and of the factors which bear upon their ability to reproduce themselves successfully; and

5. Marine mammals have proven themselves to be resources of great international significance, aesthetic and recreational as well as economic.

Jurisdiction

The NMFS Office of Protected Resources (OPR) is charged with the implementation of the Marine Mammal Protection Act (MMPA), Endangered Species Act (ESA), and the Fur Seal Act (FSA) with respect to the marine mammal species under NMFS jurisdiction. These marine mammals include whales, dolphins, porpoises, seals, and sea lions. The U.S. Fish and Wildlife Service implements programs and regulations for the remaining marine mammal species, including walruses, polar bears, sea otters, and manatees.

Taking of Marine Mammals

The term "take" as it pertains to marine mammals is statutorily defined to mean "to harass, hunt, capture, or kill, or attempt to harass, hunt, capture or kill any marine mammal." Under the 1994 amendments, the Congress statutorily defined and divided the term "harassment" to mean any act of pursuit, torment, or annoyance which either (1) has the potential to injure a marine mammal or marine mammal stock in the wild—known as a Level A Harassment; or (2) has the potential to disturb a marine mammal or marine mammal stock in the wild by causing disruption of behavioral patterns, including, but not limited to, migration, breathing, nursing, breeding, feeding, or sheltering—known as a Level B Harassment.

The MMPA established a moratorium, with certain exceptions, on the taking of marine mammals in U.S. waters and by U.S. citizens on the high seas, and on the importing of marine mammals and marine mammal products into the United States. The MMPA provides that the moratorium on taking of marine mammals can be waived for specific purposes if the taking will not disadvantage the affected species or stock. It also indicates that permits may be issued to take or import any marine mammal species, including depleted species, to conduct scientific research or to enhance the survival or recovery of a species or stock.

Permits may also be issued to allow for the taking of a marine mammal from the wild or the import of a non-depleted species for purposes of public display. These permits are very specific and designate the number and species of animals that can be taken, as well as time, date, location, and method of takings. Applications for permits are further discussed below.

Further, the MMPA's moratorium on taking does not apply to taking by any Indian, Aleut, or Eskimo who resides in Alaska and who dwells on the coast of the North Pacific Ocean or the Arctic Ocean if such taking is for subsistence purposes or for creating and selling authentic Native articles of handicrafts and clothing, and is not done in a wasteful manner.

The NMFS-OPR is the federal agency which develops and implements policies, procedures, and regulations for permits or authorizations to take marine mammals according to the MMPA as well as the ESA, and the FSA.

MARINE MAMMAL PERMITS AND AUTHORIZATIONS

Although, as set forth above, the Marine Mammal Protection Act established a moratorium on the "taking" of marine mammals and the importing of marine mammals and marine mammal products, certain activities are exempted from this moratorium. To participate in the exempt activities, permits and/or authorizations are required for marine mammal takes within U.S. waters by all U.S. or foreign citizens; and marine mammal takes on international waters by U.S. citizens only.

The activities which are exempted from the moratorium include:

1. Scientific research;

2. Enhancing the survival or recovery of a marine mammal species or stock;

3. Commercial and educational photography;

4. First-time import for public display;

5. Capture of wild marine mammals for public display;

6. Incidental take during commercial fisheries; and

7. Incidental take during non-fishery activities.

THE ENDANGERED SPECIES ACT

Congress enacted the Endangered Species Act in order to "conserve to the extent practicable the various species of fish or wildlife and plants facing extinction." They declared their authority to do so pursuant to certain existing international treaties and conventions.

The stated purpose of the Act is "to provide a means whereby the ecosystems upon which endangered species and threatened species depend may be conserved, to provide a program for the conservation of such endangered species and threatened species. . ."

The Act sets forth the procedure to be followed in determining whether a particular species or habitat is endangered or threatened. The Act also calls for the development and implementation of plans for the conservation and survival of listed endangered and threatened species, and sets forth restrictions regarding listed species.

The Act does, however, contain exemptions for the purpose of scientific experimentation pursuant to a permit issued by the Secretary—either the Secretary of the Interior or the Secretary of Commerce depending upon their jurisdiction—under established terms and conditions.

The U.S. Fish and Wildlife Service implements programs and regulations for terrestrial and freshwater species under the Endangered Species Act.The NMFS Office of Protected Resources (OPR) is charged with the implementation of the Endangered Species Act for marine and anadromous species.

The United States Fish and Wildlife Service

In carrying out its responsibilities under the Endangered Species Act, the USFWS Division of Endangered Species maintains a list of those species determined to be threatened and/or endangered. This listing process is one of the basic functions performed by the USFWS.

In order to list, reclassify, or delist a species, the USFWS must follow a strict legal process known as a "rulemaking" procedure. The rule is first proposed in the Federal Register, a U.S. government publication. After a public comment period, the USFWS decides if the rule should be approved, revised, or withdrawn. This process can take up to a year, or longer in unusual circumstances. Participation by all interested parties, including the general public, the scientific community, other government agencies, and foreign governments, is encouraged.

Once an animal or plant is listed, all protective measures authorized by the Endangered Species Act apply to the species and its habitat. Such measures include: (i) protection from any adverse effects of Federal activities; (ii) restrictions on taking, transporting, or selling a species; (iii) authorization for the USFWS to develop and carry out recovery plans; (iv) the authority to purchase important habitat; and (v) Federal aid to State and Commonwealth wildlife agencies that have cooperative agreements with the USFWS.

The USFWS has developed a priority system designed to direct its efforts toward the plants and animals in greatest need of protection. The magnitude of threat is the most important consideration, followed by the immediacy of the threat and the taxonomic distinctiveness of the species. The most distinctive is a monotypic genus, then a full species, and lastly a subspecies, variety, or vertebrate population.

The National Marine Fisheries Service

The National Marine Fisheries Service Office of Protected Resources serves as the principal liaison with environmental organizations, industry, other Federal and state agencies, and the academic community. It develops, implements, and administers programs for the protection, conservation, and recovery of species protected under the Endangered Species Act. The Office also develops and implements policies, procedures, and regulations for permits to take listed species. Additionally, the Office establishes cooperative agreements with states regarding listed species management and protection and identifies endangered species research needs to collect appropriate information for management decisions.

More detailed information concerning endangered species and animal rights may be found in this author's legal almanac entitled *Animal Rights*, also published by Oceana Publishing Company.

CHAPTER 8:
OZONE DEPLETION

THE OZONE LAYER

Ozone is a naturally occurring gas that is found in two layers of the atmosphere. As discussed in Chapter 2, in the layer surrounding the Earth's surface—the troposphere—ground-level or "bad" ozone is an air pollutant that is a key ingredient of urban smog. The troposphere extends up to the stratosphere, which is where "good" ozone protects life on Earth. Stratospheric ozone is most concentrated between 6 to 30 miles above the Earth's surface.

The stratospheric ozone layer forms a thin shield in the upper atmosphere filtering the sun's harmful ultraviolet (UV) rays. In the 1980s, scientists began accumulating evidence that the ozone layer was being depleted. It is well-established that decreases in the stratospheric ozone far above us can result in increased UV radiation reaching the Earth's surface, which in turn can lead to a greater chance of overexposure to UV radiation.

Ozone levels change from day to day and place to place but long-term decreases in the average amount of ozone have been measured over the past decade. Future levels of ozone and ultraviolet radiation will depend upon a combination of natural and manmade factors. The most common ozone-depleting chemicals are chlorofluorocarbons (CFCs).

Until recently, CFCs were used widely in industry. When CFCs are released into the air, strong winds send them up into the stratosphere where they break down and release chlorine. The chlorine attacks the ozone. According to the EPA, each chlorine atom can break apart as many as 100,000 ozone molecules during its stratospheric life.

There is international concern over the depletion of stratospheric ozone. Therefore, the United States and a number of other countries have adopted The Montreal Protocol—a treaty designed to phase out the production and use of ozone-depleting substances. Scientists predict that ozone depletion should peak between 2000 and 2010. As the international control measures reduce the release of CFCs and other ozone-depleting substances, it is expected that natural atmospheric processes will repair the ozone layer by the mid-21st century.

TYPES OF ULTRAVIOLET (UV) RADIATION

Scientists classify UV radiation into three types—UVA, UVB, and UVC. The stratospheric ozone layer absorbs some, but not all, of these types of UV radiation. UVA radiation is not absorbed by the ozone layer. UVB radiation is mostly absorbed by the ozone layer, but some does reach the Earth's surface. UVC radiation is completely absorbed by the ozone layer and oxygen.

It is the UVA and UVB radiation that reaches the Earth's surface and causes harm to human health. UVB radiation is usually associated with sunburn while UVA radiation is recognized as a deeper penetrating and more harmful radiation.

THE ULTRAVIOLET (UV) INDEX

In 1994, the U.S. Environmental Protection Agency (EPA) and the National Weather Service (NWS) introduced the UV Index as a daily report on the UV radiation levels people may experience. The Index predicts UV intensity levels on a scale of 0 to 10+, where 0 indicates a minimal risk of overexposure and 10+ means a very high risk.

Calculated on a next-day basis for dozens of cities across the United States, the UV Index takes into account clouds and other local conditions that affect the amount of UV radiation reaching the ground in different parts of the country. Although clouds do not eliminate exposure, they partially screen UV rays. By contrast, water, sand and snow all reflect UV rays, increasing exposure. However, the computation of the UV Index does not include the effects of variable surface reflection.

For more information about the UV Index, the reader can contact the EPA's Stratospheric Protection Hotline at (800) 296-1996 or visit their website at http://www.epa.gov/ozone/uvindex/stayheal.html

HEALTH EFFECTS OF UV RADIATION

UV radiation from the sun seriously threatens human health. The most immediate result is a sunburn which may cause skin to turn red, tender, become swollen and blister. A sunburn can also cause fever and nausea. Although fair-skinned individuals may be more likely to develop a sunburn, all skin types are at risk for other UV-related health effects. Too much sun exposure can change the texture of the skin, cause discolorations and premature wrinkling. Some people are more sensitive to the sun and may develop allergic reactions. Certain medications can also make a person more sensitive to the sun. Excessive sun exposure can also damage the immune system and lead to eye problems such as cornea burns and cataracts.

The most serious health effect of exposure to harmful UV rays is skin cancer, which commonly develops on the parts of the body most often exposed to the sun, such as the face, hands and arms. The three main types of skin cancer are basal cell carcinoma, squamous cell carcinoma, and malignant melanoma. Basal cell carcinomas are tumors that usually appear as small, fleshy bumps or nodules. Squamous cell carcinomas appear as nodules or as red, scaly patches. Malignant melanomas may appear without warning as a dark mole or other dark spot in the skin.

According to the Environmental Protection Agency, there has been an 1,800 percent rise in malignant melanoma since 1930. One in five Americans develops skin cancer and one American dies of skin cancer every hour. Over 1 million new cases of skin cancer are likely to be diagnosed in the United States this year. People get 80 percent of their lifetime sun exposure by the age of 18, which is why it is so important to protect children from overexposure. Health professionals have determined that early exposure in life influences the risk of developing skin cancer later in life.

CHAPTER 9:
GLOBAL WARMING AND THE GREENHOUSE EFFECT

GREENHOUSE GASES

Naturally occurring atmospheric gases include water vapor, carbon dioxide, methane, nitrous oxide, and ozone. While the energy from the sun controls the earth's weather and climate, energy from the earth is radiated back into space. These atmospheric gases are known to have heat-trapping properties—much like a "greenhouse"—which retain heat from the outgoing energy. Thus, scientists refer to these gases as "greenhouse gases."

Although this "natural" greenhouse effect is necessary to maintain a habitable temperature on earth, human activity has caused an increase in the amount of gases being released into the atmosphere. Prior to the Industrial Revolution, humans released very few gases into the atmosphere. However, industrialization has caused an unprecedented increase in the release of greenhouse gases into the atmosphere.

For example, carbon dioxide and nitrous oxide is released into the atmosphere when solid waste, fossil fuels, and wood products are burned. In fact, fossil fuels burned to run cars and trucks, heat homes and businesses, and power factories are responsible for about 98% of U.S. carbon dioxide emissions. In addition, methane is emitted during the production and transport of coal, natural gas, and oil. Nitrous oxide is emitted during agricultural and industrial activities, as well as during combustion of solid waste and fossil fuels. Added to this mix are very powerful greenhouse gases that are not naturally occurring, including hydrofluorocarbons, perfluorocarbons, and sulfur hexafluoride, which are generated in a variety of industrial processes. In 1997, the United States emitted about one-fifth of total global greenhouse gases.

CLIMATE IMPACT

Scientists have predicted that the earth's climate will change because human activities are altering the chemical composition of the atmosphere and attribute rising global temperatures to this increase in greenhouse gases. They have found that the greenhouse effect has caused the global mean surface temperatures to increase 0.5-1.0°F since the late 19th century. The 20th century's 10 warmest years all occurred in the last 15 years of the century. Scientists expect that the average global surface temperature could rise 1-4.5°F in the next fifty years, and 2.2-10°F in the next century.

Rising global temperatures are expected to have a significant impact upon the environment. Warmer temperatures could raise the sea level, and change precipitation and other local climate conditions. Changing regional climate could alter forests, agriculture, and water supplies. It could also affect human health, wildlife, and many types of habitats.

HEALTH IMPACT

It is a known fact that climate has a great impact upon the prevalence of certain diseases and other health problems. Some serious diseases are only present in warm climates. For example, mosquitoes and other insects who are active in warmer temperatures could expand their territory and increase the risk of diseases such as malaria, yellow fever, and encephalitis. Extremely hot temperatures also cause heat exhaustion and put a strain on the cardiovascular system, which can potentially impact people who have heart problems. In addition, warmer temperatures increase air and water pollution which also impacts human health, particularly those individuals who suffer from respiratory illnesses.

Warm temperatures also increase the concentration of ground level ozone—the "bad ozone." In fact, studies show that, in most of the country, an increase in air temperature of four degrees could increase ozone concentrations by about 5 percent. Ozone in the lower atmosphere damages lung tissue and causes health problems to people who suffer from asthma and other respiratory problems. Exposure to ozone can cause healthy people to suffer chest pains, nausea, and pulmonary congestion.

Studies have shown that hotter temperatures result in increased mortality rates among the elderly and the very young. Although warmer temperatures may decrease the number of people who die each year from cold weather, twice that number die from heat. Studies have shown that deaths due to heat are more sensitive to temperature changes than deaths due to the cold.

Nevertheless, because the United States has the capability to address many of these risks and concerns through various governmental and health agencies which monitor and identify infectious diseases and other health emergencies, an increase in mortality rates due to global warming in this nation are not inevitable provided the appropriate precautions are undertaken.

ENVIRONMENTAL IMPACT

The changing climate is expected to increase both evaporation and precipitation in most areas of the United States. Where evaporation increases more than precipitation, this will necessarily affect the lake and river water levels which, among other things, would cause a reduction in hydroelectric power and a decrease in water supplies. A change in water level also affects navigation. Lower water levels also increase water pollution because there is less water available to dilute the pollutants. In addition, soil will become drier and likely affect crops.

Global warming is also expected to reduce the sea ice and snow cover in the Arctic regions. The ice and snow are responsible for cooling the climate further by reflecting solar energy back into space. Without the ice and snow, the temperatures In the region would increase.

WILDLIFE IMPACT

Global warming could have many impacts on wildlife. For example, some bodies of water may become too warm for the fish that currently inhabit them. Pollution levels in the water could increase. Loss of wetlands could affect habitat and kill off the food supply of certain fish and aquatic species. Climate changes are also expected to affect birds by altering their life cycles and impacting their food supply. Scientists have already reported that rising temperatures have affected the health of polar bears and that any significant global warming would prematurely melt the sea ice. Because the bears hunt seals—their primary source of food—on the sea ice, this would lessen the time available for the bears to hunt.

GOVERNMENT ACTION

The U.S. Global Change Research Program (USGCRP) coordinates the world's most extensive research effort on climate change. Many federal agencies are actively engaged in reducing the nation's vulnerability to these types of impacts. The Federal Emergency Management Agency

(FEMA) and other agencies are reviewing structural and land-use measures for reducing vulnerability to floods. The Army Corps of Engineers and the Bureau of Reclamation are developing better ways to manage the federal system of reservoirs in the face of changing climate to meet the competing needs of navigation, hydropower, water supply, recreation, and environmental quality.

In addition, the Environmental Protection Agency (EPA) and other federal agencies are actively engaging the private sector, states, and localities in an effort to address the problem of global warming. Many cities and states have prepared greenhouse gas inventories and many are actively pursuing programs and policies that will result in greenhouse gas emission reductions.

CHAPTER 10:
CHILDREN'S HEALTH AND THE ENVIRONMENT

IN GENERAL

There is much concern over the effect of the environment on children due to their heightened susceptibility to pollutants, contaminants and carcinogens found in the air, food and water. Pound for pound, children breathe more air, drink more water, and eat more food than their adult counterparts. Because their bodies are still developing, they are less able to metabolize, detoxify and excrete pollutants. Therefore, the government has taken extra steps to try and protect children and reduce their risk of harm from these environmental contaminants.

LEGISLATION

National Agenda to Protect Children's Health from Environmental Threats

In 1995, the Environmental Protection Agency (EPA) was directed to evaluate the environmental health risks to infants and children in the United States. Pursuant to the National Agenda to Protect Children's Health from Environmental Threats, the EPA was instructed to:

1. Ensure that all standards set by the EPA are protective of any heightened risks faced by children;

2. Develop a scientific research strategy focused on the gaps in knowledge regarding child-specific susceptibility and exposure to environmental pollutants;

3. Develop new, comprehensive policies to address cumulative and simultaneous exposures faced by children;

4. Expand community right-to-know allowing families to make informed choices concerning environmental exposures to their children;

5. Encourage parental responsibility for protecting their children from environmental health threats by providing them with basic information.

6. Encourage and expand educational efforts with health care providers and environmental professionals so they can identify, prevent, and reduce environmental health threats to children; and

7. Provide the necessary funding to address children's environmental health as a top priority among relative health risks.

Executive Order

On April 21, 1997, President Clinton signed the Executive Order on the Protection of Children from Environmental Health Risks and Safety Risks. This Executive Order requires all federal agencies to assign a high priority to addressing health and safety risks to children, coordinate research priorities on children's health, and ensure that their standards take into account special risks to children. The Executive Order created a Task Force on Environmental Health Risks and Safety Risks to Children to implement the Executive Order.

The EPA Office of Children's Health Protection

In May 1997, the EPA established the Office of Children's Health Protection (OCHP) in order to implement the President's Executive Order and the National Agenda to Protect Children's Health from Environmental Threats. The stated mission of the OCHP is to make the protection of children's health a fundamental goal of public health and environmental protection in the United States.

In order to carry out its mission, the EPA has taken a number of steps to provide additional health protection for the nation's 35 million children, including increased air, water and food quality standards keeping in mind the particular susceptibilities of infants and young children.

The Environmental Protection Agency Children's Environmental Health Hotline may be reached at (877) 590-KIDS.

CHILDREN AND AIR QUALITY

Indoor Air Quality

As previously set forth in this almanac, indoor air quality can have a significant impact on health, much higher than outdoor air quality. It has also been recognized that infants and children spend much of their time indoors and are therefore particularly susceptible to the damaging effects of indoor air pollutants.

Secondhand Smoke

According to the Centers for Disease Control and Prevention's (CDC) National Center for Environmental Health reports, 43 percent of children, two months through 11 years of age, live in a home with at least one smoker. Children who live with smokers involuntarily inhale many pollutants in smoke. Secondhand smoke is a complex mixture of more than 4,000 chemicals, including carbon monoxide, nicotine, tars, formaldehyde and hydrogen cyanide, several of which are known human carcinogens or respiratory irritants.

Children exposed to secondhand smoke are more likely to develop bronchitis, pneumonia, respiratory infections, middle ear infection, and asthma symptoms. The frequency of infection depends directly on the amount of smoke in the home. For example, children who live with two smoking parents have more respiratory infections than children who live with one smoking parent. The lowest rates of respiratory infections and asthma are found in children of parents who do not smoke at all. In addition, maternal smoking during pregnancy is associated with an increased incidence of Sudden Infant Death Syndrome.

Household Allergens

Household allergens, such as house dust mites, cockroaches, pet dander, pollen, molds, spores, bacteria, and viruses, are known to cause or aggravate asthma. Allergic reactions often combine with and seriously aggravate the symptoms of asthma, the common cold, pneumonia, and other conditions. Allergens also may cause eye, nose and throat irritation, shortness of breath, dizziness, lethargy, and fever.

Volatile Organic Compounds

Volatile organic compounds are chemicals that evaporate from substances, such as cleaning products, adhesives, paints, dry-cleaning fluids, and wood preservatives. These harmful chemicals can be emitted from these products into the air and may be trapped indoors, especially in tightly sealed buildings. Symptoms of exposure to such chemicals may include eye, nose and lung irritation, rash, headache, nausea, vomiting, and asthma.

Lead Exposure

Exposure to lead-contaminated dust is the most common way to get lead poisoning. Lead is highly toxic and exposure to it can be dangerous, especially for children who are 6 or younger. The most common household lead hazards are lead-based paint, lead dust, and contaminated soil. Lead paint in older housing is the principal source of lead exposure today but drinking water can be a significant source of lead exposure in some homes and buildings. Other sources of lead hazards are older plumbing fixtures, vinyl miniblinds, painted toys and household furniture made before 1978 that may be painted with lead-based paint.

Lead is poisonous because it interferes with some of the body's basic functions. Exposure to low levels of lead can permanently affect children. In low levels, lead can cause nervous system and kidney damage, learning disabilities such as attention deficit disorder, and decreased intelligence. High levels of lead can have devastating effects on children, including brain damage, neurologic dysfunction, seizures, unconsciousness, and, in some cases, death. According to the EPA, nearly 1 million American children have elevated blood lead levels of concern.

Pesticides

According to the EPA, 75 percent of U.S. households used at least one pesticide product—such as an insecticide or disinfectant—indoors during the past year. In 1990, the American Association of Poison Control Centers reported that some 79,000 children were involved in common household pesticide poisonings or exposures. According to the EPA, exposure to high levels of cyclodiene pesticides has produced various symptoms, including headaches, dizziness, muscle twitching, weakness, tingling sensations, and nausea. In addition, the EPA is concerned that cyclodienes might cause long-term damage to the liver and the central nervous system, as well as an increased risk of cancer.

Outdoor Air Quality

Outdoor air pollution is particularly unhealthy for children. This is so because children breathe more rapidly and inhale more pollutants per pound of body weight than adults. Their airways are more narrow than those of adults and their respiratory systems are still developing. Children are also outdoors more often than adults, leading to greater exposure.

It is difficult to completely prevent exposure, but it may be possible to reduce exposure when pollutant levels are high, as levels vary from day to day and are higher during certain times of day. One way of limiting exposure is to schedule the child's outdoor activities during periods when the air quality is least harmful.

As set forth in Chapter 2, there are six major outdoor air pollutants: (i) ozone; (ii) particulate matter; (iii) carbon monoxide; (iv) lead; (v) nitrogen dioxide; and (vi) sulfur dioxide. Although the EPA has set national standards for each of these pollutants, more than 25% of the nation's children live in areas that do not meet all national air quality standards, thus efforts must be made to protect children from exposure.

Ozone

Ozone is particularly harmful to children because their respiratory systems are still developing, they breathe faster than adults, causing more of the pollutant to get to their lungs, and their airways are smaller. In addition, children spend more time outdoors and their play is often high-energy, which can increase their breathing rates ten times, and they play outdoors most in the summer, when ozone pollution is greatest.

Particulate Matter

Children are especially sensitive to particulate matter, which may cause respiratory disease because the particulate matter is inhaled and the particles accumulate in the lungs.

Carbon Monoxide

Again, in large part due to their size and developing respiratory systems, carbon monoxide is particularly dangerous to children.

Lead

In addition to the lead exposure found indoors, lead is also found in the air, soil, and water and it can be inhaled or ingested. Outdoor lead exposure is also a health concern, particularly for children, and is known to lead to brain damage and other neurological and developmental problems.

Nitrogen Dioxide

Short-term exposures leads to an increase in respiratory illness in children and long-term exposure may lead to permanent lung damage.

Sulfur Dioxide

In children with asthma, high levels of sulfur dioxide in the air can cause temporary breathing problems if they are playing outdoors. Short-term exposure may result in reduced lung function and symptoms of wheezing, chest tightness, or shortness of breath and long-term exposure may cause respiratory illness.

CHILDREN AND DRINKING WATER

There has been much concern about the safety of drinking water for children. According to the EPA, the United States has the safest drinking water system in the world. Although drinking water may contain low levels of contaminants, public water suppliers must comply with the EPA's maximum levels as set forth in the Safe Drinking Water Act. These standards, however, do not cover private wells, therefore, private well owners are responsible for making sure their drinking water is safe.

The EPA scientists conduct risk assessments for special populations, including children, that may be more vulnerable to contaminants in water. Standards for lead, nitrates and nitrites are specifically based on risk to children because they are the most vulnerable to these particular contaminants.

Risks to children are taken very seriously because children—especially infants—drink more fluid per pound of body weight than adults and the immune systems of very young children are not yet fully developed. Thus, young children are less able to fight microbial contaminants in drinking water. Some microbes may induce diarrhea and vomiting, which may cause children to become dehydrated more quickly than adults, and some chemical contaminants may affect learning, motor skills and sex hormones during important growth stages in children.

More information on contaminants in drinking water is available from the EPA's Safe Drinking Water Hotline at (800) 426-4791 or may be obtained by visiting the EPA's Safewater website at http://www.epa.gov/safewater.

In addition, to find out more about the drinking water quality in your community and state, read your water quality report. A copy of the report may be obtained from your water supplier and may also be available online.

CHILDREN AND FOOD POLLUTANTS

There is a lot of concern about the chemicals and pollutants contained in food eaten by infants and young children and the negative effects on their developing systems. Pound for pound, children eat three to four times more food than adults, thus ingesting a disproportionate amount of pollutants. This is compounded by the fact that their diet is much less varied and thus they consume a disproportionate amount of a particular potentially contaminated food item.

Food can be contaminated by a number of pollutants. For example, foods can contain lead if they are grown in soil with a high lead content. It is possible, however, to help prevent these environmental risks by ensuring that children have a balanced diet and avoid eating large quantities of food with potentially high levels of pollutants.

CHILDHOOD ASTHMA AND THE ENVIRONMENT

Asthma is a chronic inflammatory lung disease that causes airways to tighten and narrow, causing difficulty in breathing. Asthma has become a major public health problem among children over the past 15 years, and particularly among minority children and children from lower income households. Asthma results from a combination of environmental exposures and genetic and other factors.

Asthma Triggers

Common asthma "triggers" are exercise, allergies, viral infections and smoke. The "triggers" cause the airway linings to become inflamed and fill with mucus. The muscles lining the airways tighten and constrict, making them even more narrowed and obstructed. This causes coughing, wheezing, chest tightness, and shortness of breath. Reducing a child's exposure to such the asthma triggers will reduce the asthma symptoms and improve lung function.

Allergic Triggers

According to the American Medical Association, asthma may be triggered by allergens such as house dust mites; mold or yeast spores; pollen; cat hair, saliva and urine; dog hair and saliva; cockroach particles; aspirin or other nonsteroidal anti-inflammatory drugs; and metabisulfite, which is used as a preservative in many beverages and some foods.

Non-Allergic Asthma Triggers

According to the American Medical Association, non-allergic asthma triggers include tobacco smoke; smog; natural gas, propane, or kerosene used as cooking fuel; wood smoke; coal smoke; gas, wood, coal, and kerosene heating units; paint fumes; viral respiratory infections; exercise; and weather changes.

Children with asthma are also particularly sensitive to outdoor air pollutants such as ozone, sulfur dioxide, and particulate matter are respiratory irritants and can exacerbate asthma.

Childhood Asthma Statistics

According to the Environmental Protection Agency:

. 1. An estimated 4.8 million children—1 in 15—under 18 years of age have asthma.

2. Asthma rates have increased 160% in the past 15 years in children under 5 years of age.

3. Asthma is the leading chronic illness in children of the United States and the leading cause of school absenteeism due to chronic illness.

4. Almost three hundred children die each year from asthma, and 150,000 are hospitalized.

5. The cost of asthma to the U.S. economy was estimated to be $6.2 billion in 1990.

6. Asthma-related hospitalizations have risen disproportionately for inner-city children, and in particular for minority populations.

CHILDHOOD CANCER AND THE ENVIRONMENT

Cancer among children is a substantial public concern. Each year in the United States, approximately 12,400 children and adolescents younger than 20 years of age are diagnosed with cancer and approximately 2,300 children and adolescents die of cancer each year. According to the EPA, there is a need to determine whether and to what extent environmental contaminants play a role in causing some cancers in children.

Cancer is characterized by the uncontrolled growth of cells. A cancerous cell loses its ability to regulate its own growth, control cell division, and interpret messages from other cells. Carcinogens are substances that trigger or accelerate the development of cancer. It is known that exposure to certain carcinogens in the environment may be associated with some human cancers, including:

1. Secondhand smoke;

2. Radon;

3. Asbestos;

4. Ultraviolet Light;

5. Some Hazardous Waste; and

6. Some Pesticides.

For example, asbestos—a fibrous mineral used in construction materials—is present in public buildings, such as schools, and in some homes. Asbestos is known to have caused lung cancer and malignant mesothelioma in the children of asbestos workers when the children were exposed to asbestos-contaminated dust brought home from work on their parents' shoes and clothing.

The EPA also estimates that at least 1,000 premature deaths from cancer will occur in this country over the next 30 years among children who are exposed today to asbestos in schools. However, asbestos is only harmful if inhaled thus if the asbestos contained in the material is not disturbed enough to release microscopic particles into the air, it should not cause disease.

Another common carcinogen potentially affecting children is ultraviolet light from the sun. Children are particularly vulnerable because they spend so much time in the sun at play. Overexposure to the sun may damage a child's skin. According to the EPA, excessive sunburns experienced by children 10-15 years of age triples their chance of developing malignant melanoma later in life.

According to the EPA, exposure to hazardous wastes that have been released into the environment may present serious health hazards to children. Many of such hazardous wastes contain carcinogenic materials. Children may be exposed to such wastes when they play or live near uncontrolled hazardous waste sites or spills. The EPA estimates that 12 million people, including 4 million children, live within one mile of a hazardous waste site.

APPENDIX 1:
TABLE OF ACRONYMS AND ABBREVIATIONS COMMONLY USED IN ENVIRONMENTAL LAW

AAEE: American Academy of Environmental Engineers

AAP: Asbestos Action Program

AAPCO: American Association of Pesticide Control Officials

AARC: Alliance for Acid Rain Control

A&C: Abatement and Control

ACA: American Conservation Association

ACBM: Asbestos-Containing Building Material

ACE: Alliance for Clean Energy

ACEEE: American Council for an Energy Efficient Economy

ACM: Asbestos-Containing Material

ACP: Air Carcinogen Policy

ACQR: Air Quality Control Region

ACTS: Asbestos Contractor Tracking System

ACWA: American Clean Water Association

ACWM: Asbestos-Containing Waste Material

ADABA: Acceptable Data Base

ADSS: Air Data Screening System

AEA: Atomic Energy Act

AEE: Alliance for Environmental Education

AEERL: Air and Energy Engineering Research Laboratory

AEM: Acoustic Emission Monitoring

AERE: Association of Environmental and Resource Economists

AFA: American Forestry Association

AFCA: Area Fuel Consumption Allocation

AFCEE: Air Force Center for Environmental Excellence

AHERA: Asbestos Hazard Emergency Response Act

AID: Agency for International Development

AIHC: American Industrial Health Council

AL: Acceptable Level

Air Pollution Control Officers

ALARA: As Low As Reasonably Achievable

AMBIENS: Atmospheric Mass Balance of Industrially Emitted and Natural Sulfur

AMOS: Air Management Oversight System

AMPS: Automatic Mapping and Planning System

AMSA: Association of Metropolitan Sewer Agencies

ANC: Acid Neutralizing Capacity

ANPR: Advance Notice of Proposed Rulemaking

ANRHRD: Air, Noise, & Radiation Health Research Division

AOC: Abnormal Operating Conditions

AOD: Argon-Oxygen Decarbonization

AOML: Atlantic Oceanographic and Meteorological Laboratory

APA: Administrative Procedures Act

APCA: Air Pollution Control Association

APCD: Air Pollution Control District

APHA: American Public Health Association

APTI: Air Pollution Training Institute

APWA: American Public Works Association

AQCCT: Air-Quality Criteria and Control Techniques

AQCP: Air Quality Control Program

AQCR: Air-Quality Control Region

AQD: Air-Quality Digest

AQDHS: Air-Quality Data Handling System

AQDM: Air-Quality Display Model

AQMA: Air-Quality Maintenance Area

AQMP: Air-Quality Maintenance Plan

AQMP: Air-Quality Management Plan

AQSM: Air-Quality Simulation Model

AQTAD: Air-Quality Technical Assistance Demonstration

A&R: Air and Radiation

ARAR: Applicable or Relevant and Appropriate Standards, Limitations, Criteria, and Requirements

ARB: Air Resources Board

ARCC: American Rivers Conservation Council

ARCS: Alternative Remedial Contract Strategy

ARG: American Resources Group

ARIP: Accidental Release Information Program

ARL: Air Resources Laboratory

ARM: Air Resources Management

ARO: Alternate Regulatory Option

ARRP: Acid Rain Research Program

ARRPA: Air Resources Regional Pollution Assessment Model

ASDWA: Association of State Drinking Water Administrators

ASHAA: Asbestos in Schools Hazard Abatement Act

ASIWCPA: Association of State and Interstate Water Pollution Control Administrators

AST: Advanced Secondary (Wastewater) Treatment

ASTSWMO: Association of State and Territorial Solid Waste Management Officials

ATERIS: Air Toxics Exposure and Risk Information System

ATS: Action Tracking System

ATSDR: Agency for Toxic Substances and Disease Registry

ATTF: Air Toxics Task Force

A/WPR: Air/Water Pollution Report

AWT: Advanced Wastewater Treatment

AWWA: American Water Works Association

AWWARF: American Water Works Association Research Foundation.

BAC: Biotechnology Advisory Committee

BACM: Best Available Control Measures

BACT: Best Available Control Technology

BADT: Best Available Demonstrated Technology

BaP: Benzo(a)Pyrene

BART: Best Available Retrofit Technology

BAT: Best Available Technology

BATEA: Best Available Treatment Economically Achievable

BCT: Best Control Technology

BCPCT: Best Conventional Pollutant Control Technology

BDAT: Best Demonstrated Achievable Technology

BDCT: Best Demonstrated Control Technology

BDT: Best Demonstrated Technology

BMR: Baseline Monitoring Report

BO: Budget Obligations

BP: Boiling Point

BSI: British Standards Institute

BSO: Benzene Soluble Organics

BTZ: Below the Treatment Zone

BUN: Blood Urea Nitrogen

CA: Citizen Act.

CAA: Clean Air Act

CAAA: Clean Air Act Amendments

CAER: Community Awareness and Emergency Response

CAFO: Consent Agreement/Final Order

CAG: Carcinogenic Assessment Group

CAMP: Continuous Air Monitoring Program

CAO: Corrective Action Order

CAP: Criteria Air Pollutant

CAR: Corrective Action Report

CAS: Center for Automotive Safety

CAS: Chemical Abstract Service

CASAC: Clean Air Scientific Advisory Committee

CAU: Carbon Adsorption Unit

CCAA: Canadian Clean Air Act

CCAP: Center for Clean Air Policy

CD: Climatological Data

CDD: Chlorinated dibenzo-p-dioxin

CDF: Chlorinated dibenzofuran

CDS: Compliance Data System

CEA: Cooperative Enforcement Agreement CEA: Cost and Economic Assessment

CEARC: Canadian Environmental Assessment Research Council

CEB: Chemical Element Balance

CEMS: Continuous Emission Monitoring System

CEPP: Chemical Emergency Preparedness Plan

CEQ: Council on Environmental Quality

CERCLA: Comprehensive Environmental Response, Compensation, and Liability Act (1980)

CERCLIS: Comprehensive Environmental Response, Compensation, and Liability Information System

CERT: Certificate of Eligibility

CFC: Chlorofluorocarbons

CFM: Chlorofluoromethanes

CFR: Code of Federal Regulations

CIS: Chemical Information System.

CLEANS: Clinical Laboratory for Evaluation and Assessment of Toxic Substances

CM: Corrective Measure

CMEP: Critical Mass Energy Project

CNG: Compressed Natural Gas

CPF: Carcinogenic Potency Factor

CPO: Certified Project Officer

CQA: Construction Quality Assurance

CR: Continuous Radon Monitoring

CWA: Clean Water Act (aka FWPCA)

CWAP: Clean Water Action Project

CZMA: Coastal Zone Management Act

DCO: Delayed Compliance Order

DCO: Document Control Officer

DDT: DichloroDiphenylTrichloroethane

DERs: Data Evaluation Records

DES: Diethylstilbesterol

DI: Diagnostic Inspection

DMR: Discharge Monitoring Report

DNA: Deoxyribonucleic acid

DO: Dissolved Oxygen

DPD: Method of measuring chlorine residual in water

DQO: Data Quality Objective

DSAP: Data Self Auditing Program

DSCF: Dry Standard Cubic Feet

DSCM: Dry Standard Cubic Meter

DSS: Domestic Sewage Study

DWEL: Drinking Water Equivalent Level

DWS: Drinking Water Standard

EA: Environmental Audit

EAP: Environmental Action Plan

ECRA: Economic Cleanup Responsibility Act

EDB: Ethylene Dibromide

EDC: Ethylene Dichloride

EDF: Environmental Defense Fund

EDTA: Ethylene Diamine Triacetic Acid

EEA: Energy and Environmental Analysis

EERU: Environmental Emergency Response Unit

EHC: Environmental Health Committee

EHS: Extremely Hazardous Substance

EI: Emissions Inventory

EIA: Environmental Impact Assessment.

EIR: Environmental Impact Report

EIS: Environmental Impact Statement

EL: Exposure Level

ELI: Environmental Law Institute

ELR: Environmental Law Reporter

EM: Electromagnetic Conductivity

EPAA: Environmental Programs Assistance Act

EPCRA: Emergency Preparedness and Community Right to Know Act

ERAMS: Environmental Radiation Ambient Monitoring System

ERC: Emergency Response Commission

ERC: Emissions Reduction Credit

ERC: Environmental Research Center

ERCS: Emergency Response Cleanup Services

ERDA: Energy Research and Development Administration

ERD&DAA: Environmental Research, Development and Demonstration Authorization Act

ERL: Environmental Research Laboratory

ERNS: Emergency Response Notification System

ERT: Emergency Response Team

ERTAQ: ERT Air Quality Model

ES: Enforcement Strategy

ESA: Endangered Species Act

ETS: Environmental Tobacco Smoke

EUP: Experimental Use Permit

ExEx: Expected Exceedance

FACA: Federal Advisory Committee Act

FCC: Fluid Catalytic Converter

FDL: Final Determination Letter

FEDS: Federal Energy Data System

FEPCA: Federal Environmental Pesticide Control Act; enacted as amendments to FIFRA.

FERC: Federal Energy Regulatory Commission

FF: Federal Facilities

FFDCA: Federal Food, Drug, and Cosmetic Act

FIFRA: Federal Insecticide, Fungicide, and Rodenticide Act

FLM: Federal Land Manager

FLPMA: Federal Land Policy and Management Act

FOIA: Freedom Of Information Act

FP: Fine Particulate

FPA: Federal Pesticide Act

FPPA: Federal Pollution Prevention Act

FRA: Federal Register Act

FRN: Final Rulemaking Notice

FS: Feasibility Study

FUA: Fuel Use Act

FURS: Federal Underground Injection Control Reporting System

FWPCA: Federal Water Pollution and Control Act (aka CWA)

GEMS: Global Environmental Monitoring System

GIS: Global Indexing System

GLERL: Great Lakes Environmental Research Laboratory

GPG: Grams-per-Gallon

GPR: Ground-Penetrating Radar

GPS: Groundwater Protection Strategy

GR: Grab Radon Sampling

GWPS: Groundwater Protection Standard

HA: Health Advisory

HAP: Hazardous Air Pollutant

HAPEMS: Hazardous Air Pollutant Enforcement Management System

HC: Hydrocarbon

HCCPD: Hexachlorocyclo-pentadiene

HCP: Hypothermal Coal Process

HDPE: High Density Polyethylene

HEPA: High-Efficiency Particulate Air

HHE: Human Health and the Environment

HI: Hazard Index

HMTA: Hazardous Materials Transportation Act

HRUP: High-Risk Urban Problem

HSDB: Hazardous Substance Data Base

HSL: Hazardous Substance List

HSWA: Hazardous and Solid Waste Amendments

HW: Hazardous Waste

HWM: Hazardous Waste Management

ICBN: International Commission on the Biological Effects of Noise

IES: Institute for Environmental Studies

IP: Inhalable Particles

IPM: Inhalable Particulate Matter

IRM: Intermediate Remedial Measures

JAPCA: Journal of Air Pollution Control Association

LAER: Lowest Achievable Emission Rate

LAMP: Lake Acidification Mitigation Project

LD LO: The lowest dosage of a toxic substance that kills test organisms.

MOE: Margin Of Exposure

MOS: Margin of Safety

MRL: Maximum-Residue Limit

National Institute of Occupational Safety and Health

NSDWR: National Secondary Drinking Water Regulations

OCD: Offshore and Coastal Dispersion of: Optional Form

PATS: Pesticide Action Tracking System

PHC: Principal Hazardous Constituent

PHSA: Public Health Service Act

PI: Preliminary Injunction

PIRG: Public Interest Research Group

PM: Particulate Matter

PM10: Particulate Matter (nominally 10m and less)

PM15: Particulate Matter (nominally 15m and less)

PNA: Polynuclear Aromatic Hydrocarbons

PO: Project Officer

POC: Point Of Compliance

POE: Point Of Exposure

POHC: Principal Organic Hazardous Constituent

POI: Point Of Interception

POLREP:Pollution Report

POM: Particulate Organic Matter

POTW: Publicly Owned Treatment Works

PPB: Parts Per Billion

PPIC: Pesticide Programs Information Center

PPT: Parts Per Trillion

PPTH: Parts Per Thousand

PRA: Paperwork Reduction Act

PRA: Planned Regulatory Action

PRP: Potentially Responsible Party

PSC: Program Site Coordinator

PSI: Pounds Per Square Inch

PTFE: Polytetrafluoroethylene (Teflon)

PVC: Polyvinyl Chloride

PWSS: Public Water Supply System

QAC: Quality Assurance Coordinator

Quality Control

QAMIS: Quality Assurance Management and Information System

QCI: Quality Control Index

RA: Reasonable Alternative

RAMS: Regional Air Monitoring System

RAP: Radon Action Program

RAP: Reregistration Assessment Panel

REAP: Regional Enforcement Activities Plan

REE: Rare Earth Elements

REEP: Review of Environmental Effects of Pollutants

REPS: Regional Emissions Projection System

RESOLVE: Center for Environmental Conflict Resolution

RF: Response Factor

RIC: Radon Information Center

RNA: Ribonucleic Acid

RQ: Reportable Quantities

RRC: Regional Response Center

RRT: Regional Response Team

RSD: Risk-Specific Dose

RSE: Removal Site Evaluation

RTECS: Registry of Toxic Effects of Chemical Substances

RUP: Restricted Use Pesticide

S&A: Sampling and Analysis

SAIC: Special-Agents-In-Charge

SAIP: Systems Acquisition and Implementation Program

SANE: Sulfur and Nitrogen Emissions

SARA: Superfund Amendments and Reauthorization Act of 1986

SC: Sierra Club

SCAP: Superfund Consolidated Accomplishments Plan

SCBA: Self-Contained Breathing Apparatus

SCC: Source Classification Code

SCD/SWDC: Soil or Soil and Water Conservation District

SCFM: Standard Cubic Feet Per Minute

SCLDF: Sierra Club Legal Defense Fund

SCRC: Superfund Community Relations Coordinator

SCSA: Soil Conservation Society of America

SCSP: Storm and Combined Sewer Program

SDWA: Safe Drinking Water Act

SEA: State Enforcement Agreement

SEA: State/EPA Agreement

SEP: Standard Evaluation Procedures

SEPWC: Senate Environment and Public Works Committee

SERC: State Emergency Planning Commission

SES: Secondary Emissions Standard

SF: Superfund

SHWL: Seasonal High Water Level

SIP: State Implementation Plan

SITE: Superfund Innovative Technology Evaluation

SOC: Synthetic Organic Chemicals

SPS: State Permit System

SSA: Sole Source Aquifer

SV: Sampling Visit

SWDA: Solid Waste Disposal Act

SWMU: Solid Waste Management Unit

TAMS: Toxic Air Monitoring System

TAMTAC: Toxic Air Monitoring System Advisory Committee

TAPDS: Toxic Air Pollutant Data System

TAS: Tolerance Assessment System

TCDD: Dioxin (Tetrachlorodibenzo-p-dioxin)

THC: Total Hydrocarbons

TOX: Tetradichloroxylene

TPY: Tons Per Year

TQM: Total Quality Management

TSCA: Toxic Substances Control Act

TVA: Tennessee Valley Authority

TWA: Time Weighted Average

TWS: Transient Water System

TZ: Treatment Zone

UAQI: Uniform Air Quality Index

UCC: Ultra Clean Coal

UCL: Upper Control Limit

UEL: Upper Explosive Limit

UFL: Upper Flammability Limit

UIC: Underground Injection Control

UNEP: United Nations Environment Program

USDW: Underground Sources of Drinking Water

USFS: United States Forest Service

UST: Underground Storage Tank

UTP: Urban Transportation Planning

UV: Ultraviolet

UZM: Unsaturated Zone Monitoring

VE: Visual Emissions

VOC: Volatile Organic Compounds

VP: Vapor Pressure

VSD: Virtually Safe Dose

VSS: Volatile Suspended Solids

WAP: Waste Analysis Plan

WCED: World Commission on Environment and Development

WENDB: Water Enforcement National Data Base

WERL: Water Engineering Research Laboratory

WHO: World Health Organization

WHWT: Water and Hazardous Waste Team

WICEM: World Industry Conference on Environmental Management

WL: Warning Letter

WL: Working Level (radon measurement)

WPCF: Water Pollution Control

WQS: Water Quality Standard

WRC: Water Resources Council

WRDA: Water Resources Development Act

WRI: World Resources Institute

WSF: Water Soluble Fraction

WSRA: Wild and Scenic Rivers Act

WSTB: Water Sciences and Technology Board

WSTP: Wastewater Sewage Treatment Plant

WWF: World Wildlife Fund

WWTP: Wastewater Treatment Plant

WWTU: Wastewater Treatment Unit

ZRL: Zero Risk Level

SOURCE: U.S. Environmental Protection Agency

APPENDIX 2:
U.S. ENVIRONMENTAL PROTECTION AGENCY—REGIONAL OFFICES

REGION	AREAS COVERED	ADDRESS	TELEPHONE
REGION 1	CT, MA, ME, NH, RI, VT	U.S. EPA—Region 1, John F. Kennedy Federal Building, One Congress Street, Boston, MA 02203	(617) 565-3420 (617) 565-3415
REGION 2	NJ, NY, PR, VI	U.S. EPA—Region 2, 290 Broadway, New York, NY 10007	(212) 637-3000
REGION 3	DE, DC, MD, PA, VA, WV	U.S. EPA—Region 3, 841 Chestnut Street, Philadelphia, PA 19107	(215) 597-9800
REGION 4	AL, FL, GA, KY, MS, NC, SC, TN	U.S. EPA—Region 4, 345 Courtland Street NE, Atlanta, GA 30365	(404) 347-4727
REGION 5	IL, IN, MI, MN, OH, WI	U.S. EPA—Region 5, 77 West Jackson Boulevard, Chicago, IL 60604	(312) 353-2000
REGION 6	AR, LA, NM, OK, TX	U.S. EPA—Region 6, 1445 Ross Avenue, Suite 900, Dallas, TX 75202	(214) 655-6444
REGION 7	IA, KS, MO, NE	U.S. EPA—Region 7, 726 Minnesota Avenue, Kansas City, KS 66101	(913) 551-7000

REGION	AREAS COVERED	ADDRESS	TELEPHONE
REGION 8	CO, MT, ND, SD, UT, WY	U.S. EPA—Region 8, 999 18th Street, Suite 500, Denver, CO 80202	(303) 293-1603
REGION 9	AZ, CA, HI, NV, AMERICAN SAMOA, GUAM, PALAU, NORTHERN MARIANA ISLANDS	U.S. EPA—Region 9, 75 Hawthorne Street, San Francisco, CA 94105	(415) 744-1305
REGION 10	AK, ID, OR, WA	U.S. EPA—Region 10, 1200 6th Avenue, Seattle, WA 98101	(206) 553-1200

SOURCE: U.S. Environmental Protection Agency

APPENDIX 3:
U.S. ENVIRONMENTAL PROTECTION AGENCY CRIMINAL INVESTIGATION DIVISION—REGIONAL OFFICES

REGION	AREA	ADDRESS	TELEPHONE
REGION I	Boston	U.S. EPA-CID, JFK Federal Building, One Congress Street, Boston, MA 02203-2211	617-565-3636
	New Haven	U.S. EPA-CID, Robert N. Giamo Federal Building, 150 Court Street, Room 433, New Haven, CT 06507-1707	617-565-3436
REGION II	New York	U.S. EPA-CID, 290 Broadway, New York, NY 10007-1866	212- 637-3610
	Edison	U.S. EPA-CID, 2890 Woodbridge Avenue, Edison, NJ 08837	908-906-6997
	Buffalo	U.S. EPA-CID, U.S. Attorney's Office, 138 Delaware Avenue, Room 558, Buffalo NY 14202	716-551-4811
REGION III	Philadelphia	U.S. EPA-CID, 841 Chestnut Building, Philadelphia, PA 19107	215-566-2376
	Annapolis	U.S. EPA-CID, 2530 Riva Road, Suite 300, Annapolis, MD 21401	410-573-2784

REGION	AREA	ADDRESS	TELEPHONE
	Pittsburgh/Wheeling	U.S. EPA-CID, Methodist Building, 11th and Chapline Street, Room 109, Wheeling, WV 26003	304-234-0274
REGION IV	Atlanta	U.S. EPA-CID, 100 Alabama Street, Atlanta, GA 30303	404-562-9795
	Charleston	U.S. EPA-CID, P.O. Box 978, Charleston, SC 29402	803-727-4863
	Miami	U.S. EPA-CID, U.S. Attorney's Office, 99 Northeast 4th Street, Room 444, Miami, FL 33132	305-536-3000
	Nashville	U.S. EPA-CID, U.S. Attorney's Office, 450 James Robertson Parkway, Nashville, TN 37243-0485	615-741-3108
REGION V	Chicago	U.S. EPA-CID, 77 West Jackson, Chicago, IL 60604	312886-9872
	Cleveland	U.S. EPA-CID, 25089 Center Ridge Road, Westlake, OH 44145	216-835-5200
	Detroit	U.S. EPA-CID, 9311 Groh Road, Grosse Ile, MI 48138-1697	313-692-7650
	Minneapolis/St. Paul	U.S. EPA-CID, 316 North Roberts Street, Room 266, St. Paul, MN 55101	612-290-4414
	Indianapolis	U.S. EPA-CID, 46 East Ohio Street, 5th Floor, Indianapolis, ID 46204	317-226-5110
REGION VI	Dallas	U.S. EPA-CID, First Interstate Bank at Fountain Place, 1445 Ross Avenue, Suite 1200, Dallas, TX 75202	214-665-6600

REGION	AREA	ADDRESS	TELEPHONE
	Houston	U.S. EPA-CID, 440 Louisiana, Suite 1150, Houston, TX 77002-1635	713-227-1882
	Baton Rouge	U.S. EPA-CID, 750 Florida Street, Suite 300, Baton Rouge, LA 70821	504-389-0216
REGION VII	St. Louis	U.S. EPA-CID, 1222 Spruce Street, St. Louis, MO 63103	314-539-3422
	Kansas City	U.S. EPA-CID, 726 Minnesota Avenue, Kansas City, KS 66101	913-551-7060
REGION VIII	Denver	U.S. EPA-CID, 999 18th Street, Suite 500, Denver, CO 80202-2466	303-312-6876
REGION IX	San Francisco	U.S. EPA-CID, 75 Hawthorne Street, San Francisco, CA 94105-3901	415-744-2485
	Los Angeles	600 South Lake Avenue, Suite 502, Pasadena, CA 91106	818-583-7528
	Phoenix	U.S. EPA-CID, 522 N. Central, Suite 206, Phoenix, AR 85004	602-379-3809
REGION X	Seattle	U.S. EPA-CID, 1200 Six Avenue, Seattle, WA 98101	206-553-8306
	Portland	U.S. EPA-CID, 811 South West 6th Avenue, 3rd Floor, Portland OR 97204	503-326-3541

SOURCE: U.S. ENVIRONMENTAL PROTECTION AGENCY, CRIMINAL INVESTIGATION DIVISION

APPENDIX 4:
U.S. ENVIRONMENTAL PROTECTION AGENCY—DEPARTMENTAL HOTLINES

DEPARTMENT	HOTLINE NUMBER	FAX
Acid Rain Division	202-233-9620	Not supplied
EPA Air Risk Information	919-541-0888	919-541-0824
Asbestos Abatement/Management Ombudsman	800-368-5888	703-305-6462
Office of Air Quality Planning & Standards Control Technology Center	919-541-0800	919-541-0242
Electric and Magnetic Fields (EMF) Information	703-442-8934	703-821-8236
Environmental Financing Information Network (EFIN)	202-564-4994	202-565-2587
Office of Environmental Justice	800-962-6215	202-260-0852
Atmospheric Pollution Prevention Division—Green Lights Program	888-STAR-YES	202-233-9575
Hazardous Waste Ombudsman	800-262-7937	202-260-8929
Indoor Air Quality Information Clearinghouse (IAQINFO)	202-484-1307	None Supplied
Office of Inspector General—Program Management Division	202-260-4977	202-260-6976

Methods Information Communication Exchange Service (MICE)	703-821-4690	703-448-0282
National Antimicrobial Information Network	800-447-6349	541-737-0761
National Lead Information Center	800-LEADFYI	202-659-1192
National Pesticide Telecommunications Network	800-858-7378	503-737-0761
National Radon Information	800-SOS-RADON	202-293-0032
National Response Center Hotline	800-424-8802	Not Supplied
National Small Flows Clearinghouse	800-624-8301	304-293-3161
Ozone Protection	800-296-1996	Not Supplied
Pollution Prevention Information Clearinghouse (PPIC)	202-260-1023	202-260-4659
Superfund and EPCRA	800-424-9346	Not Supplied
Safe Drinking Water Hotline	800-426-4791	703-285-1101
Small Business Ombudsman	800-368-5888	703-305-6462
Stratospheric Ozone Information Hotline	800-296-1996	301-231-6377
Toxic Substances Control Act (TSCA) Assistance Information Service(TAIS)	202-554-1404	202-554-5603
Toxic Release Inventory—User Support Service	202-260-1531	202-401-2347
Wetlands Information Hotline	800-832-7828	703-525-0201

Source: U.S. Environmental Protection Agency

APPENDIX 5:
COMMON AIR POLLUTANTS

POLLUTANT	SOURCE	HEALTH EFFECTS	ENVIRONMENTAL EFFECTS
OZONE	chemical reaction of pollutants; VOCs and NOx	breathing problems, reduced lung function, asthma, irritates eyes, stuffy nose, reduced resistance to colds and other infections, may speed up aging of lung tissue	ozone can damage plants and trees; smog can cause reduced visibility
VOLATILE ORGANIC COMPOUNDS (VOCs)	released from burning fuel, solvents, paints, glues and other products used at work or at home	In addition to ozone effects, many VOCs can cause serious health problems such as cancer	In addition to ozone effects, some VOCs may harm plants
NITROGEN OXIDE	burning of gasoline, natural gas, coal, oil, etc., lung damage	illnesses of breathing passages and lungs	nitrogen dioxide is an ingredient of acid rain which can damage trees and lakes

POLLUTANT	SOURCE	HEALTH EFFECTS	ENVIRONMENTAL EFFECTS
CARBON MONOXIDE (CO)	burning of gasoline, natural gas, coal, oil, etc.	reduces ability of blood to bring oxygen to body cells and tissues; cells and tissues need oxygen to work; may be particularly hazardous to people who have heart or circulatory problems and people who have damaged lungs or breathing passages	
PARTICULATE MATTER (dust, smoke, soot)	burning of wood, diesel and other fuels; industrial plants; agriculture (plowing burning off fields); unpaved roads	nose and throat irritation, lung damage, bronchitis, early death	particulates are the main source of haze that reduces visibility
SULFUR DIOXIDE	burning of coal and oil, especially high-sulfur coal from the Eastern United States; industrial processes (paper, metals)	breathing problems, may cause permanent damage to lungs	SO2 is an ingredient in acid rain, which can damage trees and lakes

SOURCE: U.S. ENVIRONMENTAL PROTECTION AGENCY, OFFICE OF AIR QUALITY PLANNING AND STANDARDS

APPENDIX 6:
NATIONAL INFORMATION SOURCES FOR INDOOR AIR QUALITY

FEDERAL AGENCY	CONTACT INFORMATION
AMERICAN ASSOCIATION OF POISON CONTROL CENTERS (AAPCC)	(202) 872-5955
AMERICAN LUNG ASSOCIATION	(800) LUNG-USA
CENTERS FOR DISEASE CONTROL AND PREVENTION OFFICE OF LEAD POISONING	(800) 488-7330
CENTERS FOR DISEASE CONTROL AND PREVENTION OFFICE ON SMOKING AND HEALTH	(404) 488-5701
NATIONAL LEAD INFORMATION CENTER	(800) LEAD-FYI
NATIONAL PESTICIDES TELECOMMUNICATIONS NETWORK	(800) 858-PEST
NATIONAL RADON HOTLINE	(800) SOS-RADON
OCCUPATIONAL SAFETY AND HEALTH ADMINISTRATION (OSHA)	(202) 219-8151
RCRA/SUPERFUND HOTLINE	(800) 424-9346
SAFE DRINKING WATER HOTLINE	(800) 426-4791
TSCA ASSISTANCE INFORMATION SERVICE	(202) 554-1404
U.S. CONSUMER PRODUCT SAFETY COMMISSION	(800) 638-CPSC
U.S. DEPARTMENT OF HOUSING AND URBAN DEVELOPMENT	(800) 245-2691
U.S. EPA INDOOR AIR QUALITY INFORMATION CLEARINGHOUSE	(800) 438-4318
U.S. PUBLIC HEALTH SERVICE	(215) 596-1888

SOURCE: U.S. Environmental Protection Agency

APPENDIX 7:
STATE INFORMATION SOURCES FOR INDOOR AIR QUALITY

STATE	ADDRESS	CONTACT	TELEPHONE NUMBER
ALABAMA	Dept. of Public Health, P.O. Box 303017, Montgomery, AL 36130-3017	Gary Jones	(334) 206-5373
ALASKA	Dept. of Health and Social Services, Radiological Health Program, 4500 Boniface Parkway, Juneau, AK 99507-1270	Janice Adair	(907) 563-6529
ARIZONA	Radiation Regulatory Agency, 4814 S. 40th Street, Phoenix, AZ 85040	Patricia Arreola	(602) 230-5830
ARKANSAS	Dept. of Health, 4815 West Markham St., Slot 30, Little Rock, AR 72205-3867	Stan Evans	(501) 661-2986

STATE	ADDRESS	CONTACT	TELEPHONE NUMBER
CALIFORNIA	Dept. of Health Services, P.O. Box 942-732, Sacramento, CA 94234-7320	Jed Waldman	(510) 540-2469
COLORADO	Dept. of Public Health, Environment Laboratory and Radiation Services Division, 8100 Lowry Boulevard, Denver, CO 80220	Steve Fine	(303) 692-3164
CONNECTICUT	Dept. of Public Health, P.O. Box 340308, Hartford, CT 06106-4474	Brian Toal	(860) 509-7742
DELAWARE	Office of Radiation Control, P.O. Box 637, Dover, DE 19903	Maria Rejai	(302) 739-4731
DISTRICT OF COLUMBIA	Health Department, Environmental Health Administration, 51 N. St. N.E., Washington, DC 20002	Bernard Bloom	(202) 535-2989
FLORIDA	Department of Health, Bureau of Facility Programs, 4052 Bald Cypress Way, Bin A08, Tallahassee, FL 32399-1710	Tim Wallace	(850) 245-4288

STATE	ADDRESS	CONTACT	TELEPHONE NUMBER
GEORGIA	Dept. of Natural Resources, Pollution Prevention Assistance Division, 7 M.L. King Jr. Dr., Suite 450, Atlanta, GA 30334	Carl Johnson	(404) 657-6522 (404) 872-3549
HAWAII	Department of Health, Radiation Branch, 591 Ala Moana Blvd. Honolulu, HI 96813	Jerry Haruno	(808) 586-4700
IDAHO	Indoor Environment Program, P.O. Box 83720, Boise, ID 83720-0036	Russell Duke	(208) 334-4964
ILLINOIS	Dept. of Nuclear Safety, 1035 Outer Park Drive, Springfield, IL 62704	Mike Moomey	(217) 782-5830
INDIANA	State Dept. of Health, Indoor & Radiological Health, 2 North Meridian St., 5th Floor, Indianapolis, IN 46204-3003	Rudy Cansino	(317) 383-6147
IOWA	Dept. of Public Health, Lucas State Office Building, 321 E 12th Street, Des Moines, IA 50319-0075	Rick Welke	(515) 281-4928

STATE	ADDRESS	CONTACT	TELEPHONE NUMBER
KANSAS	Dept. of Health and Environment, Radiation Control Program, Forbes Field, Bldg. 283, Topeka KS 66620-0001	Gary Miller	(785) 296-1547
KENTUCKY	Dept. of Health Services, Environmental Management Branch, 275 East Main Street, Frankfort, KY 40621	n/a	(502) 573-3382
LOUISIANA	Dept. of Environmental Quality, P.O. Box 70884-2135, Baton Rouge, LA 70884-2135	Kenneth Lanier	(504) 568-8537
MAINE	Radiation Control Program, 10 State House Station, 157 Capitol Street, Augusta, ME 04333	Robert Stilwell	(207) 287-5676
MARYLAND	Dept. of the Environment, 2500 Broenig Highway, Baltimore, MD 21224	Jim Lewis	(410) 631-3801
MASSACHUSETTS	Dept. of Public Health, Radiation Control Program, 23 Service Center, Northampton, MA 01060	Howard S. Wensley	(617) 983-6761

STATE	ADDRESS	CONTACT	TELEPHONE NUMBER
MICHIGAN	Radiological Protection Section, Drinking Water and Radiological Protection Division, 815 Terminal Road, Lansing, MI 48906	David Wade	(517) 335-8037
MINNESOTA	Dept. of Health, Division of Environmental Health, P.O. Box 64975, St. Paul, MN 55164-0975	Laura Oatman	(651) 215-0909
MISSISSIPPI	Dept. of Health, Division of Radiation Health & Radon Program, 3150 Lawson Street, Jackson, MS 39213-5754	Joe Fahner	(601) 576-7411
MISSOURI	Dept. of Health, Bureau of Environmental Equity, 930 Wildwood Drive, Jefferson City, MO 65109	Daryl W. Roberts	(573) 751-6160
MONTANA	Dept. of Environmental Quality, Occupational & Radiological Health Quality, P.O. Box 20091, Helena, MT 59620-0301	Brian Green	(406) 444-6768

STATE	ADDRESS	CONTACT	TELEPHONE NUMBER
NEBRASKA	Dept. of Health and Human Services, Public Health Assurance Division, 301 Centennial Mall South, 3rd Fl, Lincoln, NE 68509 5007	Molly Goedeker,	(402) 471-8320
NEVADA	State Health Division, Radiological Health Section, 1179 Fairview Drive, Suite 102, Carson City, NV 89701-5405	David Going	(775) 687-5494
NEW HAMPSHIRE	Dept. of Radiological Health, Health & Welfare Building, Six Hazen Drive, Concord, NH 03301-6527	Teresa Ferrara	(603) 271-4676
NEW JERSEY	Dept. of Environmental Protection, Radiation Protection Program, Radon Program, 25 Arctic Parkway, P.O. Box 415, Trenton, NJ 08625	James A. Brownlee	(609) 984-2193
NEW MEXICO	Environment Dept., Community Services Bureau, 525 Camino de los Marquez, Suite 5, Sante Fe NM 87502	Millicent Edison	(505) 827-0006

STATE	ADDRESS	CONTACT	TELEPHONE NUMBER
NEW YORK	Department of Health, Center for Environmental Health, 547 River Street, Troy, NY 12180-2166	Edward G. Horn	(518) 402-7800
NORTH CAROLINA	Division of Radiation Protection, 3825 Barrett Drive, Raleigh, NC 27609-7221	Will Service	(919) 715-6431
NORTH DAKOTA	Dept. of Health, Environmental Health Section, P.O. Box 5520, Bismarck, ND 58502-5520	Jesse Green	(701) 328-5188
OHIO	Dept. of Health, Bureau of Diagnostics, Safety & Performance Certification, P.O. Box 118, Columbus, OH 43215-0118	Steve Wagner	(614) 644-7630
OKLAHOMA	Dept. of Environmental Quality, P.O. Box 1677, Oklahoma City, OK 73101-1677	Emily Allen	(405) 528-1500
OREGON	Dept. of Human Resources, Health Division, 800 NE Oregon Street, Suite 260, Portland, OR 97232	Ray D. Paris	(503) 731-4014

STATE	ADDRESS	CONTACT	TELEPHONE NUMBER
PENNSYLVANIA	Dept. of Environmental Protection, Bureau of Radiation Protection, Rachel Carson State Office Bldg., P.O. Box 8469, Harrisburg, PA 17105-8469	Ralph Scalan	(717) 787-6548
RHODE ISLAND	Dept. of Health, Office of Occupational & Radiological Health, 3 Capital Hill, Room 206, Providence, RI 02908	Robert Vanderslice	(401) 277-3424
SOUTH CAROLINA	Dept. of Health & Environmental Control, 2600 Bull Street, Columbia, SC 29201	Dianne S. Minasian	(803) 898-4467
SOUTH DAKOTA	Dept. of Environment & Natural Resources, Joe Foss Building, 523 E. Capitol, Room 217, Pierre, SD 57501	Barbara Regynski	(605) 773-3151
TENNESSEE	Dept. of Environment & Conservation, Div. of Pollution Prevention and Environmental Awareness, 401 Church Street, 8th Floor, Nashville, TN 37243-1551	Jackie L. Waynick	(615) 532-0570

STATE	ADDRESS	CONTACT	TELEPHONE NUMBER
TEXAS	Dept. of Health, Bureau of Radiological Control, 1100 West 49th Street, Austin, TX 78756	Quade R. Stahl	(512) 834-6600
UTAH	Dept. of Environmental Quality, P.O. Box 144850, Salt Lake City, UT 84114-4850	Marvin H. Maxell	(801) 536-4000
VERMONT	Dept. of Health, Division of Health Protection, 108 Cherry Street, P.O. Box 70, Burlington, VT 05402	John A. Mazzucco	(802) 863-7388
VIRGINIA	Dept. of Health, Bureau of Radiological Health, 1500 E. Main Street. Richmond, VA 23218	Nancy Saylor	(804) 762-4421
WASHINGTON	State Dept. of Health, Division of Radiation Protection, P.O. Box 47827, Olympia, WA 98504-7825	Tim Hardin	(360) 664-8860
WEST VIRGINIA	Bureau of Public Health, Office of Environmental Health Services, 815 Quarrier Street, Suite 418, Charleston, WV 25301	Anthony Turner	(304) 558-3427

STATE	ADDRESS	CONTACT	TELEPHONE NUMBER
WISCONSIN	Department of Health and Family Services, 1 West St., P.O. Box 309, Madison, WI 53701-0309	Walt Smith	(608) 266-2871
WYOMING	Dept. of Health, 2300 Capitol Avenue, Hathaway Bldg., Room 486, Cheyenne, WY 82002-0710	Gerald Blackwell	(307) 777-7394

SOURCE: U.S. Environmental Protection Agency

APPENDIX 8:
REFERENCE GUIDE OF MAJOR INDOOR AIR POLLUTANTS IN THE HOME

POLLUTANT	SOURCES	HEALTH EFFECTS	LEVELS IN HOMES	STEPS TO REDUCE EXPOSURE
RADON	Earth and rock beneath home; well water; building materials	No immediate symptoms; estimated to contribute to between 7, 000 and 30, 000 lung cancer deaths each year; smokers are at higher risk of developing radon-induced lung cancer	The average indoor radon level is 1.3 picocuries per liter (pCi/L) and the average outdoor level is about 0.4 pCi/L.	Test your home for radon; fix your home if your radon level is 4 picocuries per liter (pCi/L) or higher; radon levels less than 4 pCi/L still pose a risk and in many cases may be reduced.

POLLUTANT	SOURCES	HEALTH EFFECTS	LEVELS IN HOMES	STEPS TO REDUCE EXPOSURE
ENVIRONMENTAL TOBACCO SMOKE (Secondhand Smoke)	Cigarette, pipe, and cigar smoking	Eye, nose, and throat irritation; headaches; lung cancer; may contribute to heart disease. Specifically for children: increased risk of lower respiratory tract infections such as bronchitis and pneumonia and ear infections; build-up of fluid in the middle ear; increased severity and frequency of asthma episodes; decreased lung function	Particle levels in homes without smokers or other strong particle sources are the same as or lower than those outdoors. Homes with one or more smokers may have particle levels several times higher than outdoor levels	Do not smoke in your home or permit others to do so; do not smoke if children are present, particularly infants and toddlers; if smoking indoors cannot be avoided increase ventilation in the area where smoking takes place by opening windows or using exhaust fans.

POLLUTANT	SOURCES	HEALTH EFFECTS	LEVELS IN HOMES	STEPS TO REDUCE EXPOSURE
BIOLOGICALS	Wet or moist walls, ceilings, carpets, and furniture; poorly maintained humidifiers, dehumidifiers, and air conditioners; bedding; household pets	Eye, nose, and throat irritation; shortness of breath; dizziness; lethargy; fever; digestive problems. Can cause asthma: humidifier fever; influenza and other infectious diseases	Indoor levels of pollen and fungi are lower than outdoor levels except where indoor sources of fungi are present. Indoor levels of dust mites are higher than outdoor levels	Install and use fans vented to outdoors in kitchens and bathrooms; vent clothes dryers to outdoors; clean cool mist and ultrasonic humidifiers in accordance with manufacturer's instructions and refill with clean water daily; empty water trays in air conditioners, dehumidifiers, and refrigerators frequently; clean and dry or remove water-damaged carpets; use basements as living areas only if they are leak-proof and have adequate ventilation; use dehumidifiers to maintain humidity between 30-50 percent.

POLLUTANT	SOURCES	HEALTH EFFECTS	LEVELS IN HOMES	STEPS TO REDUCE EXPOSURE
CARBON MONOXIDE	Unvented kerosene and gas space heaters; leaking chimneys and furnaces; back-drafting from furnaces, gas water heaters, woodstoves, and fireplaces; gas stoves; automobile exhaust from attached garages; environmental tobacco smoke	At low concentrations, fatigue in healthy people and chest pain in people with heart disease; at higher concentrations, impaired vision and coordination; headaches; dizziness; confusion; nausea; can cause flu-like symptoms that clear up after leaving home; fatal at very high concentrations	Average levels in homes without gas stoves vary from 0.5 to 5 parts per million (ppm); levels near properly adjusted gas stoves are often 5 to 15 ppm and those near poorly adjusted stoves may be 30 ppm or higher	Keep gas appliances properly adjusted; consider purchasing a vented space heater when replacing an unvented one; use proper fuel in kerosene space heaters; install and use an exhaust fan vented to outdoors over gas stoves; open flues when fireplaces are in use; choose properly sized woodstoves that are certified to meet EPA emission standards; make certain that doors on all woodstoves fit tightly; have a trained professional inspect, clean, and tune-up central heating system (furnaces, flues, and chimneys) annually and repair any leaks promptly; do not idle the car inside garage.

POLLUTANT	SOURCES	HEALTH EFFECTS	LEVELS IN HOMES	STEPS TO REDUCE EXPOSURE
NITROGEN DIOXIDE	Kerosene heaters; unvented gas stoves and heaters; environmental tobacco smoke	Eye, nose, and throat irritation; may cause impaired lung function and increased respiratory infections in young children	Average level in homes without combustion appliances is about half that of outdoors; in homes with gas stoves, kerosene heaters, or unvented gas space heaters, indoor levels often exceed outdoor levels	See steps under carbon monoxide.
ORGANIC GASES	Household products including: paints, paint strippers, and other solvents; wood preservatives; aerosol sprays; cleansers and disinfectants; moth repellents and air fresheners; stored fuels and automotive products; hobby supplies; dry-cleaned clothing	Eye, nose, and throat irritation; headaches; loss of coordination; nausea; damage to liver, kidney and central nervous system; some organics can cause cancer in animals and some are suspected or known to cause cancer in humans	Studies have found that levels of several organics average 2 to 5 times higher indoors than outdoors; during and for several hours immediately after certain activities, such as paint stripping, levels may be 1,000 times background outdoor levels	Use household products according to manufacturer's directions; make sure you provide plenty of fresh air when using these products; throw away unused or little-used containers safely; buy in quantities that you will use soon; keep out of reach of children and pets; never mix household care products unless directed on the label.

POLLUTANT	SOURCES	HEALTH EFFECTS	LEVELS IN HOMES	STEPS TO REDUCE EXPOSURE
RESPIRABLE PARTICLES	Fireplaces; woodstoves; kerosene heaters; and environmental tobacco smoke	Eye, nose, and throat irritation; respiratory infections and bronchitis; lung cancer; also see effects attributable to environmental tobacco smoke	Particle levels in homes without smoking or other strong particle sources are the same as or lower than outdoor levels	Vent all furnaces to outdoors; keep doors to rest of house open when using unvented space heaters; choose properly sized woodstoves certified to meet EPA emission standards; make certain that doors on all woodstoves fit tightly; have a trained professional inspect, clean, and tune-up central heating system (furnace, flues, and chimneys) annually and repair any leaks promptly; change filters on central heating and cooling systems and air cleaners according to manufacturer's directions.

POLLUTANT	SOURCES	HEALTH EFFECTS	LEVELS IN HOMES	STEPS TO REDUCE EXPOSURE
FORMALDEHYDE	Pressed wood products (hardwood/plywood wall paneling, particleboard, fiberboard) and furniture made with these pressed wood products; urea-formaldehyde foam insulation; combustion sources and environmental tobacco smoke; durable press drapes; other textiles and glues	Eye, nose, and throat irritation; wheezing and coughing; fatigue; skin rash; severe allergic reactions; may cause cancer; also see effects attributable to organic gases	Average concentrations in older homes without urea-formaldehyde foam insulation are generally well below 0.1 (ppm) and in homes with significant amounts of new pressed wood products levels can be greater than 0.3 ppm	Use exterior-grade pressed wood products which are lower-emitting because they contain phenol resins, not urea resins; use air conditioning and dehumidifiers to maintain moderate temperature and reduce humidity levels; increase ventilation, particularly after bringing new sources of formaldehyde into the home.

POLLUTANT	SOURCES	HEALTH EFFECTS	LEVELS IN HOMES	STEPS TO REDUCE EXPOSURE
PESTICIDES	Products used to kill household pests including insecticides, termiticides, and disinfectants; products used on lawns and gardens that drift or are tracked inside the house.	Irritation to eye, nose, and throat; damage to central nervous system and kidney; increased risk of cancer	Preliminary research shows widespread presence of pesticide residues in homes	Use strictly according to manufacturer's directions; mix or dilute outdoors; apply only in recommended quantities; increase ventilation when using indoors; take plants or pets outdoors when applying pesticides to them; use non-chemical methods of pest control where possible; select pest control company carefully; do not store unneeded pesticides inside home and dispose of unwanted containers safely; store clothes with moth repellents in separately ventilated areas if possible; keep indoor spaces clean, dry, and well ventilated to avoid pest and odor problems.

POLLUTANT	SOURCES	HEALTH EFFECTS	LEVELS IN HOMES	STEPS TO REDUCE EXPOSURE
ASBESTOS	Deteriorating, damaged, or disturbed insulation, fireproofing, acoustical materials, and floor tiles	No immediate symptoms but long-term risk of chest and abdominal cancers and lung diseases; smokers are at higher risk of developing asbestos-induced lung cancer	Elevated levels can occur in homes where asbestos-containing materials are damaged or disturbed	It is best to leave undamaged asbestos material alone if it is not likely to be disturbed; use trained and qualified contractors for control measures that may disturb asbestos and for cleanup.; follow proper procedures in replacing woodstove door gaskets that may contain asbestos.

POLLUTANT	SOURCES	HEALTH EFFECTS	LEVELS IN HOMES	STEPS TO REDUCE EXPOSURE
LEAD	Lead-based paint; contaminated soil, dust, and drinking water.	Lead affects practically all systems within the body; at high levels (lead levels at or above 80 micrograms per deciliter of blood) can cause convulsions, coma, and even death; lower levels of lead can cause adverse health effects on the central nervous system, kidney, and blood cells; blood lead levels as low as 10 ug/dl can impair mental and physical development	n/a	Keep areas where children play as dust-free and clean as possible; leave lead-based paint undisturbed if it is in good condition; do not sand or burn off paint that may contain lead; do not remove lead paint yourself; do not bring lead dust into the home; if your work or hobby involves lead, change clothes and use doormats before entering your home; eat a balanced diet rich in calcium and iron.

SOURCE: U.S. Environmental Protection Agency

APPENDIX 9:
STATE SOURCES FOR RADON
INFORMATION

STATE	AGENCY	ADDRESS	CONTACT	TELEPHONE NUMBER
ALABAMA	Dept. of Public Health	P.O. Box 303017, Montgomery, AL 36130-3017	James McNees	(334) 206-5391
ALASKA	Dept. of Health and Social Services, Radiological Health Program	4500 Boniface Parkway, Juneau, AK 99507-1270	Richard Seifert	(907) 474-7201
ARIZONA	Radiation Regulatory Agency	4814 S. 40th Street, Phoenix, AZ 85040	John Stewart	(602) 255-4845
ARKANSAS	Dept. of Health	4815 West Markham St., Slot 30, Little Rock, AR 72205-3867	Steve Mack	(501) 661-2301
CALIFORNIA	Dept. of Health Services	P.O. Box 942-732, Sacramento, CA 94234-7320	J. Dave Quinton	(916) 324-2208

STATE	AGENCY	ADDRESS	CONTACT	TELEPHONE NUMBER
COLORADO	Dept. of Public Health, Environment Laboratory and Radiation Services Division	8100 Lowry Boulevard, Denver, CO 80220	Linda Martin	(303) 692-3090
CONNECTI CUT	Dept. of Public Health	P.O. Box 340308, Hartford, CT 06106-4474	Frank Homiski	(860) 509-7367
DELAWARE	Office of Radiation Control	P.O. Box 637, Dover, DE 19903	Dr. Ramney Koul	(302) 739-4731
DISTRICT OF COLUMBIA	Health Department, Environmental Health Administration	51 N. St. N.E., Washington, DC 20002	Keith Keemer	(202) 535-2999
FLORIDA	Department of Health, Bureau of Facility Programs	4052 Bald Cypress Way, Bin A08, Tallahassee, FL 32399-1710	N. Michael Gilley	(850) 245-4288
GEORGIA	Dept. of Natural Resources, Pollution Prevention Assistance Division	7 M.L. King Jr. Dr., Suite 450, Atlanta, GA 30334	David Gipson	(404) 872-3549
HAWAII	Department of Health, Radiation Branch	591 Ala Moana Blvd. Honolulu, HI 96813	Russell Takata	(808) 586-4700
IDAHO	Indoor Environment Program	P.O. Box 83720, Boise, ID 83720-0036	Kara Bishop	(208) 332-7319

STATE	AGENCY	ADDRESS	CONTACT	TELEPHONE NUMBER
ILLINOIS	Dept. of Nuclear Safety	1035 Outer Park Drive, Springfield, IL 62704	Marjorie Walle	(217) 785-9958
INDIANA	State Dept. of Health, Indoor & Radiological Health	2 North Meridian St., 5th Floor, Indianapolis, IN 46204-3003	Mary Stiker	(317) 233-7147
IOWA	Dept. of Public Health	Lucas State Office Building, 321 E 12th Street, Des Moines, IA 50319-0075	Don Flater	(515) 281-4928
KANSAS	Dept. of Health and Environment, Radiation Control Program	Forbes Field, Bldg. 283, Topeka KS 66620-0001	Kim Steves	(785) 296-1561
KENTUCKY	Dept. of Health Services, Environmental Management Branch	275 East Main Street, Frankfort, KY 40621	Douglas L. Jackson	(502) 564-4856
LOUISIANA	Dept. of Environmental Quality	P.O. Box 70884-2135, Baton Rouge, LA 70884-2135	Matt Schlenker	(225) 925-7042
MAINE	Radiation Control Program	10 State House Station, 157 Capitol Street, Augusta, ME 04333	Robert Stilwell	(207) 287-5676

STATE	AGENCY	ADDRESS	CONTACT	TELEPHONE NUMBER
MARYLAND	Dept. of the Environment	2500 Broenig Highway, Baltimore, MD 21224	Maryland does not have a radon program	n/a
MASSACHU SETTS	Dept. of Public Health, Radiation Control Program	23 Service Center, Northampto n, MA 01060	Roger Perras	(413) 586-7525
MICHIGAN	Radiological Protection Section, Drinking Water and Radiological Protection Division	815 Terminal Road, Lansing, MI 48906	Sue Hendershott	(517) 335-8037
MINNESOTA	Dept. of Health, Division of Environmental Health	P.O. Box 64975, St. Paul, MN 55164-0975	Laura Oatman	(651) 215-0909
MISSISSIPPI	Dept. of Health, Division of Radiation Health & Radon Program	3150 Lawson Street, Jackson, MS 39213-5754	Silas Anderson	(601) 987-6893
MISSOURI	Dept. of Health, Bureau of Environmental Equity	930 Wildwood Drive, Jefferson City, MO 65109	Gary McNutt	(573) 751-6160
MONTANA	Dept. of Environmental Quality, Occupational & Radiological Health Quality	P.O. Box 20091, Helena, MT 59620-0301	Brian Green	(406) 444-6768

STATE	AGENCY	ADDRESS	CONTACT	TELEPHONE NUMBER
NEBRASKA	Dept. of Health and Human Services, Public Health Assurance Division	301 Centennial Mall South, 3rd Fl, Lincoln, NE 68509-5007	Michael Benjamin	(402) 471-0594
NEVADA	State Health Division, Radiological Health Section	1179 Fairview Drive, Suite 102, Carson City, NV 89701-5405	Adian Howe	(775) 687-5394
NEW HAMPSHIRE	Dept. of Radiological Health	Health & Welfare Building, Six Hazen Drive, Concord, NH 03301-6527	David Chase	(603) 271-4674
NEW JERSEY	Dept. of Environmental Protection, Radiation Protection Program, Radon Program	25 Arctic Parkway, P.O. Box 415, Trenton, NJ 08625	Anita Kopera	(609) 984-5425
NEW MEXICO	Environment Dept.	Community Services Bureau, 525 Camino de los Marquez, Suite 5, Sante Fe NM 87502	Jeanne-Marie Crockett	(505) 476-8531
NEW YORK	Department of Health, Center for Environmental Health	547 River Street, Troy, NY 12180-2166	Dr. Salme-Alfie	(518) 402-7556

STATE	AGENCY	ADDRESS	CONTACT	TELEPHONE NUMBER
NORTH CAROLINA	Division of Radiation Protection	3825 Barrett Drive, Raleigh, NC 27609-7221	Dr. Felix Fong	(919) 571-4141
NORTH DAKOTA	Dept. of Health, Environmental Health Section	P.O. Box 5520, Bismarck, ND 58502-5520	Sandi Washek	(701) 328-5188
OHIO	Dept. of Health, Bureau of Diagnostics, Safety & Performance Certification	P.O. Box 118, Columbus, OH 43215-0118	Mark Needham	(614) 644-2727
OKLAHOMA	Dept. of Environmental Quality	P.O. Box 1677, Oklahoma City, OK 73101-1677	Jerry Matthews	(405) 702-5165
OREGON	Dept. of Human Resources, Health Division	800 NE Oregon Street, Suite 260, Portland, OR 97232	Ray D. Paris	(503) 731-4014
PENNSYLVANIA	Dept. of Environmental Protection, Bureau of Radiation Protection	Rachel Carson State Office Bldg., P.O. Box 8469, Harrisburg, PA 17105-8469	Mike Pyles	(717) 783-3594
RHODE ISLAND	Dept. of Health, Office of Occupational & Radiological Health	3 Capital Hill, Room 206, Providence, RI 02908	Edmond Arcand	(401) 222-2438

STATE	AGENCY	ADDRESS	CONTACT	TELEPHONE NUMBER
SOUTH CAROLINA	Dept. of Health & Environmental Control	2600 Bull Street, Columbia, SC 29201	Reggie Massey	(864) 241-1090
SOUTH DAKOTA	Dept. of Environment & Natural Resources	Joe Foss Building, 523 E. Capitol, Room 217, Pierre, SD 57501	Barbara Regynski	(605) 773-3151
TENNESSEE	Dept. of Environment & Conservation, Div. of Pollution Prevention and Environmental Awareness	401 Church Street, 8th Floor, Nashville, TN 37243-1551	Marsha White	(615) 299-9725
TEXAS	Dept. of Health, Bureau of Radiological Control	1100 West 49th Street, Austin, TX 78756	Gary L. Smith	(512) 834-6688
UTAH	Dept. of Environmental Quality	P.O. Box 144850, Salt Lake City, UT 84114-4850	John Hultquist	(801) 536-4250
VERMONT	Dept. of Health, Division of Health Protection	108 Cherry Street, P.O. Box 70, Burlington, VT 05402	Patricia Jacobson	(802) 865-7730
VIRGINIA	Dept. of Health, Bureau of Radiological Health	1500 E. Main Street, Richmond, VA 23218	Leslie Foldesi	(804) 786-5932
WASHINGTON	State Dept. of Health, Division of Radiation Protection	P.O. Box 47827, Olympia, WA 98504-7825	John Erickson	(360) 236-3253

STATE	AGENCY	ADDRESS	CONTACT	TELEPHONE NUMBER
WEST VIRGINIA	Bureau of Public Health, Office of Environmental Health Services	815 Quarrier Street, Suite 418, Charleston, WV 25301	Beattie Debord	(304) 558-3427
WISCONSIN	Department of Health and Family Services	1 West St., P.O. Box 309, Madison, WI 53701-0309	Conrad Weiffenbach	(608) 267-4796
WYOMING	Dept. of Health	2300 Capitol Avenue, Hathaway Bldg., Room 486, Cheyenne, WY 82002-0710	Debi Nelson	(307) 777-6015

Source: U.S. Environemental Protection Agency

APPENDIX 10:
THE SAFE DRINKING WATER ACT
(42 U.S.C. §§ 300f et seq.)

SECTION 300F. DEFINITIONS

For purposes of this title:

(1) The term "primary drinking water regulation" means a regulation which—

(A) applies to public water systems;

(B) specifies contaminants which, in the judgment of the Administrator,may have any adverse effect on the health of persons;

(C) specifies for each such contaminant either—

(i) a maximum contaminant level, if, in the judgment of the Administrator, it is economically and technologically feasible to ascertain the level of such contaminant in water in public water systems, or

(ii) if, in the judgment of the Administrator, it is not economically or technologically feasible to so ascertain the level of such contaminant, each treatment technique known to the Administrator which leads to a reduction in the level of such contaminant sufficient to satisfy the requirements of section 1412 [42 USCS § 300g-1]; and

(D) contains criteria and procedures to assure a supply of drinking water which dependably complies with such maximum contaminant levels; including accepted methods for quality control and testing procedures to insure compliance with such levels and to insure proper operation and maintenance of the system, and requirements as to (i) the minimum quality of water which may be taken into the system and (ii) siting for new facilities for public water systems.

At any time after promulgation of a regulation referred to in this paragraph, the Administrator may add equally effective quality control and testing procedures by guidance published in the Federal Register. Such procedures shall be treated as an alternative for public water systems to the quality control and testing procedures listed in the regulation.

(2) The term "secondary drinking water regulation" means a regulation which applies to public water systems and which specifies the maximum contaminant levels which, in the judgment of the Administrator, are requisite to protect the public welfare. Such regulations may apply to any contaminant in drinking water

(A) which may adversely affect the odor or appearance of such water and consequently may cause a substantial number of the persons served by the public water system providing such water to discontinue its use, or

(B) which may otherwise adversely affect the public welfare. Such regulations may vary according to geographic and other circumstances.

(3) The term "maximum contaminant level" means the maximum permissible level of a contaminant in water which is delivered to any user of a public water system.

(4) Public water system.

(A) In general. The term "public water system" means a system for the provision to the public of water for human consumption through pipes or other constructed conveyances, if such system has at least fifteen service connections or regularly serves at least twenty-five individuals. Such term includes

(i) any collection, treatment, storage, and distribution facilities under control of the operator of such system and used primarily in connection with such system, and

(ii) any collection or pretreatment storage facilities not under such control which are used primarily in connection with such system.

(B) Connections.

(i) In general. For purposes of subparagraph (A), a connection to a system that delivers water by a constructed conveyance other than a pipe shall not be considered a connection, if—

(I) the water is used exclusively for purposes other than residential uses (consisting of drinking, bathing, and cooking, or other similar uses);

(II) the Administrator or the State (in the case of a State exercising primary enforcement responsibility for public water systems) determines that alternative water to achieve the equivalent level of public health protection provided by the applicable national primary drinking water regulation is provided for residential or similar uses for drinking and cooking; or

(III) the Administrator or the State (in the case of a State exercising primary enforcement responsibility for public water systems) determines that the water provided for residential or similar uses for drinking, cooking, and bathing is centrally treated or treated at the point of entry by the provider, a pass-through entity, or the user to achieve the equivalent level of protection provided by the applicable national primary drinking water regulations.

(ii) Irrigation districts. An irrigation district in existence prior to May 18, 1994, that provides primarily agricultural service through a piped water system with only incidental residential or similar use shall not be considered to be a public water system if the system or the residential or similar users of the system comply with subclause (II) or (III) of clause (i).

(C) Transition period. A water supplier that would be a public water system only as a result of modifications made to this paragraph by the Safe Drinking Water Act Amendments of 1996 shall not be considered a public water system for purposes of the Act until the date that is two years after the date of enactment of this subparagraph [enacted Aug. 6, 1996]. If a water supplier does not serve 15 service connections (as defined in subparagraphs (A) and (B)) or 25 people at any time after the conclusion of the 2-year period, the water supplier shall not be considered a public water system.

(5) The term "supplier of water" means any person who owns or operates a public water system.

(6) The term "contaminant" means any physical, chemical, biological, or radiological substance or matter in water.

(7) The term "Administrator" means the Administrator of the Environmental Protection Agency.

(8) The term "Agency" means the Environmental Protection Agency.

(9) The term "Council" means the National Drinking Water Advisory Council established under section 1446 [42 USCS § 300j-5].

(10) The term "municipality" means a city, town, or other public body created by or pursuant to State law, or an Indian Tribe.

(11) The term "Federal agency" means any department, agency, or instrumentality of the United States.

(12) The term "person" means an individual, corporation, company, association, partnership, State, municipality, or Federal agency (and includes officers, employees, and agents of any corporation, company, association, State, municipality, or Federal agency).

(13) (A) Except as provided in subparagraph (B), the term "State" includes, in addition to the several States, only the District of Columbia, Guam, the Commonwealth of Puerto Rico, the Northern Mariana Islands, the Virgin Islands, American Samoa, and the Trust Territory of the Pacific Islands.

(B) For purposes of section 1452 [42 USCS § 300j-12], the term "State" means each of the 50 States, the District of Columbia, and the Commonwealth of Puerto Rico.

(14) The term "Indian Tribe" means any Indian tribe having a Federally recognized governing body carrying out substantial governmental duties and powers over any area. For purposes of section 1452 [42 USCS § 300j-12], the term includes any Native village (as defined in section 3(c) of the Alaska Native Claims Settlement Act (43 U.S.C. § 1602(c))).

(15) Community water system. The term "community water system" means a public water system that—

(A) serves at least 15 service connections used by year-round residents of the area served by the system; or

(B) regularly serves at least 25 year-round residents.

(16) Noncommunity water system. The term "noncommunity water system" means a public water system that is not a community water system.

SECTION 300G. COVERAGE

Subject to sections 1415 and 1416 [42 USCS §§ 300g-4, 300g-5], national primary drinking water regulations under this part [42 USCS §§ 300g et seq] shall apply to each public water system in each State; except that such regulations shall not apply to a public water system—

(1) which consists only of distribution and storage facilities (and does not have any collection and treatment facilities);

(2) which obtains all of its water from, but is not owned or operated by, a public water system to which such regulations apply;

(3) which does not sell water to any person; and

(4) which is not a carrier which conveys passengers in interstate commerce.

SECTION 300G-1. NATIONAL DRINKING WATER REGULATIONS

(a) National primary drinking water regulations; maximum contaminant level goals; simultaneous publication of regulations and goals.

(1) Effective on the enactment of the Safe Drinking Water Act Amendments of 1986 [enacted June 19, 1986], each national interim or revised primary drinking water regulation promulgated under this section before such enactment shall be deemed to be a national primary drinking water regulation under subsection (b). No such regulation shall be required to comply with the standards set forth in subsection (b)(4) unless such regulation is amended to establish a different maximum contaminant level after the enactment of such amendments.

(2) After the enactment of the Safe Drinking Water Act Amendments of 1986 [enacted June 19, 1986] each recommended maximum contaminant level published before the enactment of such amendments shall be treated as a maximum contaminant level goal.

(3) Whenever a national primary drinking water regulation is proposed under subsection (b) for any contaminant, the maximum contaminant level goal for such contaminant shall be proposed simultaneously. Whenever a national primary drinking water regulation is promulgated under subsection (b) for any contaminant, the maximum contaminant level goal for such contaminant shall be published simultaneously.

(4) Paragraph (3) shall not apply to any recommended maximum contaminant level published before the enactment of the Safe Drinking Water Act Amendments of 1986 [enacted June 19, 1986].

(b) Standards.

(1) Identification of contaminants for listing.

(A) General authority. The Administrator shall, in accordance with the procedures established by this subsection, publish a maximum contaminant level goal and promulgate a national primary drinking water regulation for a contaminant (other than a contaminant referred to in paragraph (2) for which a national primary drinking water regulation has been promulgated as of the date of enactment of the Safe Drinking Water Act Amendments of 1996 [enacted Aug. 6, 1996]) if the Administrator determines that—

(i) the contaminant may have an adverse effect on the health of persons;

(ii) the contaminant is known to occur or there is a substantial likelihood that the contaminant will occur in public water systems with a frequency and at levels of public health concern; and

(iii) in the sole judgment of the Administrator, regulation of such contaminant presents a meaningful opportunity for health risk reduction for persons served by public water systems.

(B) Regulation of unregulated contaminants.

(i) Listing of contaminants for consideration.

(I) Not later than 18 months after the date of enactment of the Safe Drinking Water Act Amendments of 1996 [enacted Aug. 6, 1996] and every 5 years thereafter, the Administrator, after consultation with the scientific community, including the Science Advisory Board, after notice and opportunity for public comment, and after considering the occurrence data base established under section 1445(g) [42 USCS § 300j-4(g)], shall publish a list of contaminants which, at the time of publication, are not subject to any proposed or promulgated national primary drinking water regulation, which are known or anticipated to occur in public water systems, and which may require regulation under this title [42 USCS §§ 300f et seq.].

(II) The unregulated contaminants considered under subclause (I) shall include, but not be limited to, substances referred to in section 101(14) of the Comprehensive Environmental Response, Compensation, and Liability Act of 1980 [42 USCS § 9601(14)], and substances registered as pesticides under the Federal Insecticide, Fungicide, and Rodenticide Act.

(III) The Administrator's decision whether or not to select an unregulated contaminant for a list under this clause shall not be subject to judicial review.

(ii) Determination to regulate.

(I) Not later than 5 years after the date of enactment of the Safe Drinking Water Act Amendments of 1996 [enacted Aug. 6, 1996], and every 5 years thereafter, the Administrator shall, after notice of the preliminary determination and opportunity for public comment, for not fewer than 5 contaminants included on the list published under clause (i), make determinations of whether or not to regulate such contaminants.

(II) A determination to regulate a contaminant shall be based on findings that the criteria of clauses (i), (ii), and (iii) of subparagraph (A) are satisfied. Such findings shall be based on the best available public health information, including the occurrence data base established under section 1445(g) [42 USCS § 300j-4(g)].

(III) The Administrator may make a determination to regulate a contaminant that does not appear on a list under clause (i) if the determination to regulate is made pursuant to subclause (II).

(IV) A determination under this clause not to regulate a contaminant shall be considered final agency action and subject to judicial review.

(iii) Review. Each document setting forth the determination for a contaminant under clause (ii) shall be available for public comment at such time as the determination is published.

(C) Priorities. In selecting unregulated contaminants for consideration under subparagraph (B), the Administrator shall select contaminants that present the greatest public health concern. The Administrator, in making such selection, shall take into consideration, among other factors of public health concern, the effect of such contaminants upon subgroups that comprise a meaningful portion of the general population (such as infants, children, pregnant women, the elderly, individuals with a history of serious illness, or other subpopulations) that are identifiable as being at greater risk of adverse health effects due to exposure to contaminants in drinking water than the general population.

(D) Urgent threats to public health. The Administrator may promulgate an interim national primary drinking water regulation for a contaminant without making a determination for the contaminant under paragraph (4)(C), or completing the analysis under paragraph (3)(C), to address an urgent threat to public health as determined by the Administrator after consultation with and written response to any comments provided by the Secretary of Health and Human Services, acting through the director of the Centers for Disease Control and Prevention or the director of the National Institutes of Health. A determination for any contaminant in accordance with paragraph (4)(C) subject to an interim regulation under this subparagraph shall be issued, and a completed analysis meeting the requirements of paragraph (3)(C) shall be published, not later than 3 years after the date on which the regulation is promulgated and the regulation shall be repromulgated, or revised if appropriate, not later than 5 years after that date.

(E) Regulation. For each contaminant that the Administrator determines to regulate under subparagraph (B), the Administrator shall publish maximum contaminant level goals and promulgate, by rule, national primary drinking water regulations under this subsection. The Administrator shall propose the maximum contaminant level goal and national primary drinking water regulation for a contaminant not later than 24 months after the determination to regulate under subparagraph (B), and may publish such proposed regulation concurrent with the determination to regulate. The Administrator shall publish a maximum contaminant level goal and promulgate a national primary drinking water regulation within 18 months after the proposal thereof. The Administrator, by notice in the Federal Register, may extend the deadline for such promulgation for up to 9 months.

(F) Health advisories and other actions. The Administrator may publish health advisories (which are not regulations) or take other appropriate actions for contaminants not subject to any national primary drinking water regulation.

(2) Schedules and deadlines.

(A) In general. In the case of the contaminants listed in the Advance Notice of Proposed Rulemaking published in volume 47, Federal Register, page 9352, and in volume 48, Federal Register, page 45502, the Administrator shall publish maximum contaminant level goals and promulgate national primary drinking water regulations—

(i) not later than 1 year after June 19, 1986, for not fewer than 9 of the listed contaminants;

(ii) not later than 2 years after June 19, 1986, for not fewer than 40 of the listed contaminants; and

(iii) not later than 3 years after June 19, 1986, for the remainder of the listed contaminants.

(B) Substitution of contaminants. If the Administrator identifies a drinking water contaminant the regulation of which, in the judgment of the Administrator, is more likely to be protective of public health (taking into account the schedule for regulation under subparagraph (A)) than a contaminant referred to in subparagraph (A), the Administrator may publish a maximum contaminant level goal and promulgate a national primary drinking water regulation for the identified contaminant in lieu of regulating the contaminant referred to in subparagraph (A). Substitutions may be made for not more than 7 contaminants referred to in subparagraph (A). Regulation of a contaminant identified under this subparagraph shall be in accordance with the schedule applicable to the contaminant for which the substitution is made.

(C) Disinfectants and disinfection byproducts. The Administrator shall promulgate an Interim Enhanced Surface Water Treatment Rule, a Final Enhanced Surface Water Treatment Rule, a Stage I Disinfectants and Disinfection Byproducts Rule, and a Stage II Disinfectants and Disinfection Byproducts Rule in accordance with the schedule published in volume 59, Federal Register, page 6361 (February 10, 1994), in table III.13 of the proposed Information Collection Rule. If a delay occurs with respect to the promulgation of any rule in the schedule referred to in this subparagraph, all subsequent rules shall be completed as expeditiously as practicable but no later than a revised date that reflects the interval or intervals for the rules in the schedule.

(3) Risk assessment, management, and communication.

(A) Use of science in decisionmaking. In carrying out this section, and, to the degree that an Agency action is based on science, the Administrator shall use—

(i) the best available, peer-reviewed science and supporting studies conducted in accordance with sound and objective scientific practices; and

(ii) data collected by accepted methods or best available methods (if the reliability of the method and the nature of the decision justifies use of the data).

(B) Public information. In carrying out this section, the Administrator shall ensure that the presentation of information on public health effects is comprehensive, informative, and understandable. The Administrator shall, in a document made available to the public in support of a regulation promulgated under this section, specify, to the extent practicable—

(i) each population addressed by any estimate of public health effects;

(ii) the expected risk or central estimate of risk for the specific populations;

(iii) each appropriate upper-bound or lower-bound estimate of risk;

(iv) each significant uncertainty identified in the process of the assessment of public health effects and studies that would assist in resolving the uncertainty; and

(v) peer-reviewed studies known to the Administrator that support, are directly relevant to, or fail to support any estimate of public health effects and the methodology used to reconcile inconsistencies in the scientific data.

(C) Health risk reduction and cost analysis.

(i) Maximum contaminant levels. When proposing any national primary drinking water regulation that includes a maximum contaminant level, the Administrator shall, with respect to a maximum contaminant level that is being considered in accordance with paragraph (4) and each alternative maximum contaminant level that is being considered pursuant to paragraph (5) or (6)(A), publish, seek public comment on, and use for the purposes of paragraphs (4), (5), and (6) an analysis of each of the following:

(I) Quantifiable and nonquantifiable health risk reduction benefits for which there is a factual basis in the rulemaking record to conclude that such benefits are likely to occur as the result of treatment to comply with each level.

(II) Quantifiable and nonquantifiable health risk reduction benefits for which there is a factual basis in the rulemaking record to conclude that such benefits are likely to occur from reductions in co-occurring contaminants that may be attributed solely to compliance with the maximum contaminant level, excluding benefits resulting from compliance with other proposed or promulgated regulations.

(III) Quantifiable and nonquantifiable costs for which there is a factual basis in the rulemaking record to conclude that such costs are likely to occur solely as a result of compliance with the maximum contaminant level, including monitoring, treatment, and other costs and excluding costs resulting from compliance with other proposed or promulgated regulations.

(IV) The incremental costs and benefits associated with each alternative maximum contaminant level considered.

(V) The effects of the contaminant on the general population and on groups within the general population such as infants, children, pregnant women, the elderly, individuals with a history of serious illness, or other subpopulations that are identified as likely to be at greater risk of adverse health effects due to exposure to contaminants in drinking water than the general population.

(VI) Any increased health risk that may occur as the result of compliance, including risks associated with co-occurring contaminants.

(VII) Other relevant factors, including the quality and extent of the information, the uncertainties in the analysis supporting subclauses (I) through (VI), and factors with respect to the degree and nature of the risk.

(ii) Treatment techniques. When proposing a national primary drinking water regulation that includes a treatment technique in accordance with paragraph (7)(A), the Administrator shall publish and seek public comment on an analysis of the health risk reduction benefits and costs likely to be experienced as the result of compliance with the treatment technique and alternative treatment techniques that are being considered, taking into account, as appropriate, the factors described in clause (i).

(iii) Approaches to measure and value benefits. The Administrator may identify valid approaches for the measurement and valuation of benefits under this subparagraph, including approaches to identify consumer willingness to pay for reductions in health risks from drinking water contaminants.

(iv) Authorization. There are authorized to be appropriated to the Administrator, acting through the Office of Ground Water and Drinking Water, to conduct studies, assessments, and analyses in support of regulations or the development of methods, $35,000,000 for each of fiscal years 1996 through 2003.

(4) Goals and standards.

(A) Maximum contaminant level goals. Each maximum contaminant level goal established under this subsection shall be set at the level at which no known or anticipated adverse effects on the health of persons occur and which allows an adequate margin of safety.

(B) Maximum contaminant levels. Except as provided in paragraphs (5) and (6), each national primary drinking water regulation for a contaminant for which a maximum contaminant level goal is established under this subsection shall specify a maximum contaminant level for such contaminant which is as close to the maximum contaminant level goal as is feasible.

(C) Determination. At the time the Administrator proposes a national primary drinking water regulation under this paragraph, the Administrator shall publish a determination as to whether the benefits of the maximum contaminant level justify, or do not justify, the costs based on the analysis conducted under paragraph (3)(C).

(D) Definition of feasible. For the purposes of this subsection, the term "feasible" means feasible with the use of the best technology, treatment techniques and other means which the Administrator finds, after examination for efficacy under field conditions and not solely under laboratory conditions, are available (taking cost into consideration). For the purpose of this paragraph, granular activated carbon is feasible for the control of synthetic organic chemicals, and any technology, treatment technique, or other means found to be the best available for the control of synthetic organic chemicals must be at least as effective in controlling synthetic organic chemicals as granular activated carbon.

(E) Feasible technologies.

(i) In general. Each national primary drinking water regulation which establishes a maximum contaminant level shall list the technology, treatment techniques, and other means which the Administrator finds to be feasible for purposes of meeting such maximum contaminant level, but a regulation under this subsection shall not require that any specified technology, treatment technique, or other means be used for purposes of meeting such maximum contaminant level.

(ii) List of technologies for small systems. The Administrator shall include in the list any technology, treatment technique, or other means that is affordable, as determined by the Administrator in consultation with the States, for small public water systems serving—

(I) a population of 10,000 or fewer but more than 3,300;

(II) a population of 3,300 or fewer but more than 500; and

(III) a population of 500 or fewer but more than 25; and that achieves compliance with the maximum contaminant level or treatment technique, including packaged or modular systems and point-of-entry or point-of-use treatment units. Point-of-entry and point-of-use treatment units shall be owned, controlled and maintained by the public water system or by a person under contract with the public water system to ensure proper operation and maintenance and compliance with the maximum contaminant level or treatment technique and equipped with mechanical warnings to ensure that customers are automatically notified of operational problems.

The Administrator shall not include in the list any point-of-use treatment technology, treatment technique, or other means to achieve compliance with a maximum contaminant level or treatment technique requirement for a microbial contaminant (or an indicator of a microbial contaminant). If the American National Standards Institute has issued product standards applicable to a specific type of point-of-entry or point-of-use treatment unit, individual units of that type shall not be accepted for compliance with a maximum contaminant level or treatment technique requirement unless they are independently certified in accordance with such standards. In listing any technology, treatment technique, or other means pursuant to this clause, the Administrator shall consider the quality of the source water to be treated.

(iii) List of technologies that achieve compliance. Except as provided in clause (v), not later than 2 years after the date of enactment of this clause [enacted Aug. 6, 1996] and after consultation with the States, the Administrator shall issue a list of technologies that achieve compliance with the maximum contaminant level or treatment technique for each category of public water systems described in subclauses (I), (II), and (III) of clause (ii) for each national primary drinking water regulation promulgated prior to the date of enactment of this paragraph [enacted Aug. 6, 1996].

(iv) Additional technologies. The Administrator may, at any time after a national primary drinking water regulation has been promulgated, supplement the list of technologies describing additional or new or innovative treatment technologies that meet the requirements of this paragraph for categories of small public water systems described in subclauses (I), (II), and (III) of clause (ii) that are subject to the regulation.

(v) Technologies that meet surface water treatment rule. Within one year after the date of enactment of this clause [enacted Aug. 6, 1996], the Administrator shall list technologies that meet the Surface Water Treatment Rule for each category of public water systems described in subclauses (I), (II), and (III) of clause (ii).

(5) Additional health risk considerations.

(A) In general. Notwithstanding paragraph (4), the Administrator may establish a maximum contaminant level for a contaminant at a level other than the feasible level, if the technology, treatment techniques, and other means used to determine the feasible level would result in an increase in the health risk from drinking water by—

(i) increasing the concentration of other contaminants in drinking water; or

(ii) interfering with the efficacy of drinking water treatment techniques or processes that are used to comply with other national primary drinking water regulations.

(B) Establishment of level. If the Administrator establishes a maximum contaminant level or levels or requires the use of treatment techniques for any contaminant or contaminants pursuant to the authority of this paragraph—

(i) the level or levels or treatment techniques shall minimize the overall risk of adverse health effects by balancing the risk from the contaminant and the risk from other contaminants the concentrations of which may be affected by the use of a treatment technique or process that would be employed to attain the maximum contaminant level or levels; and

(ii) the combination of technology, treatment techniques, or other means required to meet the level or levels shall not be more stringent than is feasible (as defined in paragraph (4)(D)).

(6) Additional health risk reduction and cost considerations.

(A) In general. Notwithstanding paragraph (4), if the Administrator determines based on an analysis conducted under paragraph (3)(C) that the benefits of a maximum contaminant level promulgated in accordance with paragraph

(4) would not justify the costs of complying with the level, the Administrator may, after notice and opportunity for public comment, promulgate a maximum contaminant level for the contaminant that maximizes health risk reduction benefits at a cost that is justified by the benefits.

(B) Exception. The Administrator shall not use the authority of this paragraph to promulgate a maximum contaminant level for a contaminant, if the benefits of compliance with a national primary drinking water regulation for the contaminant that would be promulgated in accordance with paragraph (4) experienced by—

(i) persons served by large public water systems; and

(ii) persons served by such other systems as are unlikely, based on information provided by the States, to receive a variance under section 1415(e) [42 USCS § 300g-4(e)] (relating to small system variances); would justify the costs to the systems of complying with the regulation. This subparagraph shall not apply if the contaminant is found almost exclusively in small systems eligible under section 1415(e) [42 USCS § 300g-4(e)] for a small system variance.

(C) Disinfectants and disinfection byproducts. The Administrator may not use the authority of this paragraph to establish a maximum contaminant level in a Stage I or Stage II national primary drinking water regulation (as described in paragraph (2)(C)) for contaminants that are disinfectants or disinfection byproducts, or to establish a maximum contaminant level or treatment technique requirement for the control of cryptosporidium. The authority of this paragraph may be used to establish regulations for the use of disinfection by systems relying on ground water sources as required by paragraph (8).

(D) Judicial review. A determination by the Administrator that the benefits of a maximum contaminant level or treatment requirement justify or do not justify the costs of complying with the level shall be reviewed by the court pursuant to section 1448 [42 USCS § 300j-7] only as part of a review of a final national primary drinking water regulation that has been promulgated based on the determination and shall not be set aside by the court under that section unless the court finds that the determination is arbitrary and capricious.

(7) (A) The Administrator is authorized to promulgate a national primary drinking water regulation that requires the use of a treatment technique in lieu of establishing a maximum contaminant level, if the Administrator makes a finding that it is not economically or technologically feasible to ascertain the level of the contaminant. In such case, the Administrator shall identify those treatment techniques which, in the Administrator's judgment, would prevent known or anticipated adverse effects on the health of persons to the extent feasible. Such regulations shall specify each treatment technique known to the Administrator which meets the requirements of this paragraph, but the Administrator may grant a variance from any specified treatment technique in accordance with section 1415(a)(3) [42 USCS § 300g-4(a)(3)].

(B) Any schedule referred to in this subsection for the promulgation of a national primary drinking water regulation for any contaminant shall apply in the same manner if the regulation requires a treatment technique in lieu of establishing a maximum contaminant level.

(C) (i) Not later than 18 months after the enactment of the Safe Drinking Water Act Amendments of 1986 [enacted June 19, 1986], the Administrator shall propose and promulgate national primary drinking water regulations specifying criteria under which filtration (including coagulation and sedimentation, as appropriate) is required as a treatment technique for public water systems supplied by surface water sources. In promulgating such rules, the Administrator shall consider the quality of source waters, protection afforded by watershed management, treatment practices (such as disinfection and length of water storage) and other factors relevant to protection of health.

(ii) In lieu of the provisions of section 1415 [42 USCS § 300g-4] the Administrator shall specify procedures by which the State determines which public water systems within its jurisdiction shall adopt filtration under the criteria of clause (i). The State may require the public water system to provide studies or other information to assist in this determination. The procedures shall provide notice and opportunity for public hearing on this determination. If the State determines that filtration is required, the State shall prescribe a schedule for compliance by the public water system with the filtration requirement. A schedule shall require compliance within 18 months of a determination made under clause (iii).

(iii) Within 18 months from the time that the Administrator establishes the criteria and procedures under this subparagraph, a State with primary enforcement responsibility shall adopt any necessary regulations to implement this subparagraph. Within 12 months of adoption of such regulations the State shall make determinations regarding filtration for all the public water systems within its jurisdiction supplied by surface waters.

(iv) If a State does not have primary enforcement responsibility for public water systems, the Administrator shall have the same authority to make the determination in clause (ii) in such State as the State would have under that clause. Any filtration requirement or schedule under this subparagraph shall be treated as if it were a requirement of a national primary drinking water regulation.

(v) As an additional alternative to the regulations promulgated pursuant to clauses (i) and (iii), including the criteria for avoiding filtration contained in 40 CFR 141.71, a State exercising primary enforcement responsibility for public water systems may, on a case-by-case basis, and after notice and opportunity for public comment, establish treatment requirements as an alternative to filtration in the case of systems having uninhabited, undeveloped watersheds in consolidated ownership, and having control over access to, and activities in, those watersheds, if the State determines (and the Administrator concurs) that the quality of the source water and the alternative treatment requirements established by the State ensure greater removal or inactivation efficiencies of pathogenic organisms for which national primary drinking water regulations have been promulgated or that are of public health concern than would be achieved by the combination of filtration and chlorine disinfection (in compliance with this section).

(8) Disinfection. At any time after the end of the 3-year period that begins on the date of enactment of the Safe Drinking Water Act Amendments of 1996 [enacted Aug. 6, 1996], but not later than the date on which the Administrator promulgates a Stage II rulemaking for disinfectants and disinfection byproducts (as described in paragraph (2)(C)), the Administrator shall also promulgate national primary drinking water regulations requiring disinfection as a treatment technique for all public water systems, including surface water systems and, as necessary, ground water systems. After consultation with the States, the Administrator shall (as part of the regulations) promulgate criteria that the Administrator, or a State that has primary enforcement responsibility under section 1413 [42 USCS § 300g-2], shall apply to determine whether disinfection shall be required as a treatment technique for any public water system served by ground water. The Administrator shall simultaneously promulgate a rule specifying criteria that will be used by the Administrator (or delegated State authorities) to grant variances from this requirement according to the provisions of sections 1415(a)(1)(B) and 1415(a)(3) [42 USCS § 300g-4(a)(1)(B), (a)(3)]. In implementing section 1442(e) [42 USCS § 300j-1(e)] the Administrator or the delegated State authority shall, where appropriate, give special consideration to providing technical assistance to small public water systems in complying with the regulations promulgated under this paragraph.

(9) Review and revision. The Administrator shall, not less often than every 6 years, review and revise, as appropriate, each national primary drinking water regulation promulgated under this title [42 USCS §§ 300f et seq.]. Any revision of a national primary drinking water regulation shall be promulgated in accordance with this section, except that each revision shall maintain, or provide for greater, protection of the health of persons.

(10) Effective date. A national primary drinking water regulation promulgated under this section (and any amendment thereto) shall take effect on the date that is 3 years after the date on which the reg-

ulation is promulgated unless the Administrator determines that an earlier date is practicable, except that the Administrator, or a State (in the case of an individual system), may allow up to 2 additional years to comply with a maximum contaminant level or treatment technique if the Administrator or State (in the case of an individual system) determines that additional time is necessary for capital improvements.

(11) No national primary drinking water regulation may require the addition of any substance for preventive health care purposes unrelated to contamination of drinking water.

(12) Certain contaminants.

(A) Arsenic.

(i) Schedule and standard. Notwithstanding the deadlines set forth in paragraph (1), the Administrator shall promulgate a national primary drinking water regulation for arsenic pursuant to this subsection, in accordance with the schedule established by this paragraph.

(ii) Study plan. Not later than 180 days after the date of enactment of this paragraph [enacted Aug. 6, 1996], the Administrator shall develop a comprehensive plan for study in support of drinking water rulemaking to reduce the uncertainty in assessing health risks associated with exposure to low levels of arsenic. In conducting such study, the Administrator shall consult with the National Academy of Sciences, other Federal agencies, and interested public and private entities.

(iii) Cooperative agreements. In carrying out the study plan, the Administrator may enter into cooperative agreements with other Federal agencies, State and local governments, and other interested public and private entities.

(iv) Proposed regulations. The Administrator shall propose a national primary drinking water regulation for arsenic not later than January 1, 2000.

(v) Final regulations. Not later than January 1, 2001, after notice and opportunity for public comment, the Administrator shall promulgate a national primary drinking water regulation for arsenic.

(vi) Authorization. There are authorized to be appropriated $2,500,000 for each of fiscal years 1997 through 2000 for the studies required by this paragraph.

(B) Sulfate.

(i) Additional study. Prior to promulgating a national primary drinking water regulation for sulfate, the Administrator and the Director of the Centers for Disease Control and Prevention shall jointly conduct an additional study to establish a reliable dose-response relationship for the adverse human health effects that may result from exposure to sulfate in drinking water, including the health effects that may be experienced by groups within the general population (including infants and travelers) that are potentially at greater risk of adverse health effects as the result of such exposure. The study shall be conducted in consultation with interested States, shall be based on the best available, peer-reviewed science and supporting studies conducted in accordance with sound and objective scientific practices, and shall be completed not later than 30 months after the date of enactment of the Safe Drinking Water Act Amendments of 1996 [enacted Aug. 6, 1996].

(ii) Determination. The Administrator shall include sulfate among the 5 or more contaminants for which a determination is made pursuant to paragraph (3)(B) not later than 5 years after the date of enactment of the Safe Drinking Water Act Amendments of 1996 [enacted Aug. 6, 1996].

(iii) Proposed and final rule. Notwithstanding the deadlines set forth in paragraph (2), the Administrator may, pursuant to the authorities of this subsection and after notice and opportunity for public comment, promulgate a final national primary drinking water regulation for sulfate. Any such regulation shall include requirements for public notification and options for the provision of alternative water supplies to populations at risk as a means of complying with the regulation in lieu of a best available treatment technology or other means.

(13) Radon in drinking water.

(A) National primary drinking water regulation. Notwithstanding paragraph (2), the Administrator shall withdraw any national primary drinking water regulation for radon proposed prior to the date of enactment of this paragraph [enacted Aug. 6, 1996] and shall propose and promulgate a regulation for radon under this section, as amended by the Safe Drinking Water Act Amendments of 1996.

(B) Risk assessment and studies.

(i) Assessment by NAS. Prior to proposing a national primary drinking water regulation for radon, the Administrator shall arrange for the National Academy of Sciences to prepare a risk assessment for radon in drinking water using the best available science in accordance with the requirements of paragraph (3). The risk assessment shall consider each of the risks associated with exposure to radon from drinking water and consider studies on the health effects of radon at levels and under conditions likely to be experienced through residential exposure. The risk assessment shall be peer-reviewed.

(ii) Study of other measures. The Administrator shall arrange for the National Academy of Sciences to prepare an assessment of the health risk reduction benefits associated with various mitigation measures to reduce radon levels in indoor air. The assessment may be conducted as part of the risk assessment authorized by clause (i) and shall be used by the Administrator to prepare the guidance and approve State programs under subparagraph (G).

(iii) Other organization. If the National Academy of Sciences declines to prepare the risk assessment or studies required by this subparagraph, the Administrator shall enter into a contract or cooperative agreement with another independent, scientific organization to prepare such assessments or studies.

(C) Health risk reduction and cost analysis. Not later than 30 months after the date of enactment of this paragraph [enacted Aug. 6, 1996], the Administrator shall publish, and seek public comment on, a health risk reduction and cost analysis meeting the requirements of paragraph (3)(C) for potential maximum contaminant levels that are being considered for radon in drinking water. The Administrator shall include a response to all significant public comments received on the analysis with the preamble for the proposed rule published under subparagraph (D).

(D) Proposed regulation. Not later than 36 months after the date of enactment of this paragraph [enacted Aug. 6, 1996], the Administrator shall propose a maximum contaminant level goal and a national primary drinking water regulation for radon pursuant to this section.

(E) Final regulation. Not later than 12 months after the date of the proposal under subparagraph (D), the Administrator shall publish a maximum contaminant level goal and promulgate a national primary drinking water regulation for radon pursuant to this section based on the risk assessment prepared pursuant to subparagraph (B) and the health risk reduction and cost analysis published pursuant to subparagraph (C). In considering the risk assessment and the health risk reduction and cost analysis in connection with the promulgation of such a standard, the Administrator shall take into account the costs and benefits of control programs for radon from other sources.

(F) Alternative maximum contaminant level. If the maximum contaminant level for radon in drinking water promulgated pursuant to subparagraph (E) is more stringent than necessary to reduce the contribution to radon in indoor air from drinking water to a concentration that is equivalent to the national average concentration of radon in outdoor air, the Administrator shall, simultaneously with the promulgation of such level, promulgate an alternative maximum contaminant level for radon that would result in a contribution of radon from drinking water to radon levels in indoor air equivalent to the national average concentration of radon in outdoor air. If the Administrator promulgates an alternative maximum contaminant level under this subparagraph, the Administrator shall, after notice and opportunity for public comment and in consultation with the States, publish guidelines for State programs, including criteria for multimedia measures to mitigate radon levels in indoor air, to be used by the States in preparing programs under subparagraph (G). The guidelines shall take into account data from existing radon mitigation programs and the assessment of mitigation measures prepared under subparagraph (B).

(G) Multimedia radon mitigation programs.

(i) In general. A State may develop and submit a multimedia program to mitigate radon levels in indoor air for approval by the Administrator under this subparagraph. If, after notice and the opportunity for public comment, such program is approved by the Administrator, public water systems in the State may comply with the alternative maximum contaminant level promulgated under subparagraph (F) in lieu of the maximum contaminant level in the national primary drinking water regulation promulgated under subparagraph (E).

(ii) Elements of programs. State programs may rely on a variety of mitigation measures including public education, testing, training, technical assistance, remediation grant and loan or incentive programs, or other regulatory or nonregulatory measures. The effectiveness of elements in State programs shall be evaluated by the Administrator based on the assessment prepared by the National Academy of Sciences under subparagraph (B) and the guidelines published by the Administrator under subparagraph (F).

(iii) Approval. The Administrator shall approve a State program submitted under this paragraph if the health risk reduction benefits expected to be achieved by the program are equal to or greater than the health risk reduction benefits that would be achieved if each public water system in the State complied with the maximum contaminant level promulgated under subparagraph (E). The Administrator shall approve or disapprove a program submitted under this paragraph within 180 days of receipt. A program that is not disapproved during such period shall be deemed approved. A program that is disapproved may be modified to address the objections of the Administrator and be resubmitted for approval.

(iv) Review. The Administrator shall periodically, but not less often than every 5 years, review each multimedia mitigation program approved under this subparagraph to determine whether it continues to meet the requirements of clause (iii) and shall, after written notice to the State and an opportunity for the State to correct any deficiency in the program, withdraw approval of programs that no longer comply with such requirements.

(v) Extension. If, within 90 days after the promulgation of an alternative maximum contaminant level under subparagraph (F), the Governor of a State submits a letter to the Administrator committing to develop a multimedia mitigation program under this subparagraph, the effective date of the national primary drinking water regulation for radon in the State that would be applicable under paragraph (10) shall be extended for a period of 18 months.

(vi) Local programs. In the event that a State chooses not to submit a multimedia mitigation program for approval under this subparagraph or has submitted a program that has been disapproved, any public water system in the State may submit a program for approval by the Administrator according to the same criteria, conditions, and approval process that would apply to a State program. The Administrator shall approve a multimedia mitigation program if the health risk reduction benefits expected to be achieved by the program are equal to or greater than the health risk reduction benefits that would result from compliance by the public water system with the maximum contaminant level for radon promulgated under subparagraph (E).

(14) Recycling of filter backwash. The Administrator shall promulgate a regulation to govern the recycling of filter backwash water within the treatment process of a public water system. The Administrator shall promulgate such regulation not later than 4 years after the date of enactment of the Safe Drinking Water Act Amendments of 1996 [enacted Aug. 6, 1996] unless such recycling has been ad-

dressed by the Administrator's Enhanced Surface Water Treatment Rule prior to such date.

(15) Variance technologies.

(A) In general. At the same time as the Administrator promulgates a national primary drinking water regulation for a contaminant pursuant to this section, the Administrator shall issue guidance or regulations describing the best treatment technologies, treatment techniques, or other means (referred to in this paragraph as "variance technology") for the contaminant that the Administrator finds, after examination for efficacy under field conditions and not solely under laboratory conditions, are available and affordable, as determined by the Administrator in consultation with the States, for public water systems of varying size, considering the quality of the source water to be treated. The Administrator shall identify such variance technologies for public water systems serving—

(i) a population of 10,000 or fewer but more than 3,300;

(ii) a population of 3,300 or fewer but more than 500; and

(iii) a population of 500 or fewer but more than 25, if, considering the quality of the source water to be treated, no treatment technology is listed for public water systems of that size under paragraph (4)(E). Variance technologies identified by the Administrator pursuant to this paragraph may not achieve compliance with the maximum contaminant level or treatment technique requirement of such regulation, but shall achieve the maximum reduction or inactivation efficiency that is affordable considering the size of the system and the quality of the source water. The guidance or regulations shall not require the use of a technology from a specific manufacturer or brand.

(B) Limitation. The Administrator shall not identify any variance technology under this paragraph, unless the Administrator has determined, considering the quality of the source water to be treated and the expected useful life of the technology, that the variance technology is protective of public health.

(C) Additional information. The Administrator shall include in the guidance or regulations identifying variance technologies under this paragraph any assumptions supporting the public health determination referred to in subparagraph (B), where such assumptions concern the public water system to which the technology may be applied, or its source waters. The Administrator shall provide any assumptions used in determining affordability, taking into consideration the number of persons served by such systems. The Administrator shall provide as much reliable information as practicable on performance, effectiveness, limitations, costs, and other relevant factors including the applicability of variance technology to waters from surface and underground sources.

(D) Regulations and guidance. Not later than 2 years after the date of enactment of this paragraph [enacted Aug. 6, 1996] and after consultation with the States, the Administrator shall issue guidance or regulations under subparagraph (A) for each national primary drinking water regulation promulgated prior to the date of enactment of this paragraph [enacted Aug. 6, 1996] for which a variance may be granted under section 1415(e) [42 USCS § 300g-4(e)]. The Administrator may, at any time after a national primary drinking water regulation has been promulgated, issue guidance or regulations describing additional variance technologies. The Administrator shall, not less often than every 7 years, or upon receipt of a petition supported by substantial information, review variance technologies identified under this paragraph. The Administrator shall issue revised guidance or regulations if new or innovative variance technologies become available that meet the requirements of this paragraph and achieve an equal or greater reduction or inactivation efficiency than the variance technologies previously identified under this subparagraph. No public water system shall be required to replace a variance technology during the useful life of the technology for the sole reason that a more efficient variance technology has been listed under this subparagraph.

(c) Secondary regulations; publication of proposed regulations; promulgation; amendments. The Administrator shall publish proposed national secondary drinking water regulations within 270 days after the date of enactment of this title [enacted Dec. 16, 1974]. Within 90 days after publication of any such regulation, he shall promulgate such regulation with such modifications as he deems appropriate. Regulations under this subsection may be amended from time to time.

(d) Regulations; public hearings; administrative consultations. Regulations under this section shall be prescribed in accordance with section 553 of title 5, United States Code (relating to rule-making), except that the Administrator shall provide opportunity for public hearing prior to promulgation of such regulations. In proposing and promulgating regulations under this section, the Administrator shall consult with the Secretary and the National Drinking Water Advisory Council.

(e) Science Advisory Board comments. The Administrator shall request comments from the Science Advisory Board (established under the Environmental Research, Development, and Demonstration Act of 1978) prior to proposal of a maximum contaminant level goal and national primary drinking water regulation. The Board shall respond, as it deems appropriate, within the time period applicable for promulgation of the national primary drinking water standard concerned. This subsection shall, under no circumstances, be used to delay final promulgation of any national primary drinking water standard.

SECTION 300I-1. TAMPERING WITH PUBLIC WATER SYSTEMS

(a) Tampering. Any person who tampers with a public water system shall be imprisoned for not more than 5 years, or fined in accordance with title 18 of the United States Code, or both.

(b) Attempt or threat. Any person who attempts to tamper, or makes a threat to tamper, with a public drinking water system be imprisoned for not more than 3 years, or fined in accordance with title 18 of the United States Code, or both.

(c) Civil penalty. The Administrator may bring a civil action in the appropriate United States district court (as determined under the provisions of title 28 of the United States Code) against any person who tampers, attempts to tamper, or makes a threat to tamper with a public water system. The court may impose on such person a civil penalty of not more than $ 50,000 for such tampering or not more than $ 20,000 for such attempt or threat.

(d) "Tamper" defined. For purposes of this section, the term "tamper" means—

(1) to introduce a contaminant into a public water system with the intention of harming persons; or

(2) to otherwise interfere with the operation of a public water system with the intention of harming persons.

SECTION 300J-5. NATIONAL DRINKING WATER ADVISORY COUNCIL

(a) Establishment; membership; representation of interests; term of office, vacancies; reappointment. There is established a National Drink Water Advisory Council which shall consist of fifteen members appointed by the Administrator after consultation with the Secretary. Five members shall be appointed from the general public; five members shall be appointed from appropriate State and local agencies concerned with water hygiene and public water supply; and five members shall be appointed from representatives of private organizations or groups demonstrating an active interest in the field of water hygiene and public water supply, of which two such members shall be associated with small, rural public water systems. Each member of the Council shall hold office for a term of three years, except that—

(1) any member appointed to fill a vacancy occurring prior to the expiration of the term for which his predecessor was appointed shall be appointed for the remainder of such term; and

(2) the terms of the members first taking office shall expire as follows: Five shall expire three years after the date of enactment of this title [enacted Dec. 16, 1974], five shall expire two years after such date, and five shall expire one year after such date, as designated by the Administrator at the time of appointment. The members of the Council shall be eligible for reappointment.

(b) Functions. The Council shall advise, consult with, and make recommendations to, the Administrator on matters relating to activities, functions, and policies of the Agency under this title [42 USCS §§ 300f et seq.].

(c) Compensation and allowances; travel expenses. Members of the Council appointed under this section shall, while attending meetings or conferences of the Council or otherwise engaged in business of the Council, receive compensation and allowances at a rate to be fixed by the Administrator, but not exceeding the daily equivalent of the annual rate of basic pay in effect for grade GS-18 of the General Schedule for each day (including traveltime) during which they are engaged in the actual performance of duties vested in the Council. While away from their homes or regular places of business in the performance of services for the Council, members of the Council shall be allowed travel expenses, including per diem in lieu of subsistence, in the same manner as persons employed intermittently in the Government service are allowed expenses under section 5703(b) of title 5 of the United States Code.

(d) Advisory committee termination provision inapplicable. Section 14(a) of the Federal Advisory Committee Act (relating to termination) [5 USCS Appx. § 14(a)] shall not apply to the Council.

SECTION 300J-6. FEDERAL AGENCIES

(a) In general. Each department, agency, and instrumentality of the executive, legislative, and judicial branches of the Federal Government—

(1) owning or operating any facility in a wellhead protection area;

(2) engaged in any activity at such facility resulting, or which may result, in the contamination of water supplies in any such area;

(3) owning or operating any public water system; or

(4) engaged in any activity resulting, or which may result in, underground injection which endangers drinking water (within the meaning of section 1421(d)(2) [42 USCS § 300h(d)(2)]), shall be subject to, and comply with, all Federal, State, interstate, and local requirements, both substantive and procedural (including any requirement for permits or reporting or any provisions for injunctive relief and such sanctions as may be imposed by a court to enforce such relief), respecting the protection of such wellhead areas, respecting such public water systems, and respecting any underground injection in the same manner and to the same extent as any person is subject to such requirements, including the payment of reasonable service charges. The Federal, State, interstate, and local substantive and procedural requirements referred to in this subsection include, but are not limited to, all administrative orders and all civil and administrative penalties and fines, regardless of whether such penalties or fines are punitive or coercive in nature or are imposed for isolated, intermittent, or continuing violations. The United States hereby expressly waives any immunity otherwise applicable to the United States with respect to any such substantive or procedural requirement (including, but not limited to, any injunctive relief, administrative order or civil or administrative penalty or fine referred to in the preceding sentence, or reasonable service charge). The reasonable service charges referred to in this subsection include, but are not limited to, fees or charges assessed in connection with the processing and issuance of permits, renewal of permits, amendments to permits, review of plans, studies, and other documents, and inspection and monitoring of facilities, as well as any other nondiscriminatory charges that are assessed in connection with a Federal, State, interstate, or local regulatory program respecting the protection of wellhead areas or public water systems or respecting any underground injection. Neither the United States, nor any agent, employee, or officer thereof, shall be immune or exempt from any process or sanction of any State or Federal Court with respect to the enforcement of any such injunctive relief. No agent, employee, or officer of the United States shall be personally liable for any civil penalty under any Federal, State, interstate, or local law concerning the protection of wellhead areas or public water systems or concerning underground injection with respect to any act or omission within the scope of the official duties of the agent, employee, or officer. An agent, employee, or officer of the United States shall be subject to any criminal sanction (including, but not limited to, any fine or imprisonment) under any Federal or State requirement adopted pursuant to this title, but no department, agency, or instrumentality of the executive, legisla-

tive, or judicial branch of the Federal Government shall be subject to any such sanction. The President may exempt any facility of any department, agency, or instrumentality in the executive branch from compliance with such a requirement if he determines it to be in the paramount interest of the United States to do so. No such exemption shall be granted due to lack of appropriation unless the President shall have specifically requested such appropriation as a part of the budgetary process and the Congress shall have failed to make available such requested appropriation. Any exemption shall be for a period not in excess of 1 year, but additional exemptions may be granted for periods not to exceed 1 year upon the President's making a new determination. The President shall report each January to the Congress all exemptions from the requirements of this section granted during the preceding calendar year, together with his reason for granting each such exemption.

(b) Administrative penalty orders.

(1) In general. If the Administrator finds that a Federal agency has violated an applicable requirement under this title [42 USCS §§ 300f et seq.], the Administrator may issue a penalty order assessing a penalty against the Federal agency.

(2) Penalties. The Administrator may, after notice to the agency, assess a civil penalty against the agency in an amount not to exceed $25,000 per day per violation.

(3) Procedure. Before an administrative penalty order issued under this subsection becomes final, the Administrator shall provide the agency an opportunity to confer with the Administrator and shall provide the agency notice and an opportunity for a hearing on the record in accordance with chapters 5 and 7 of title 5, United States Code [5 USCS §§ 501 et seq., 701 et seq.].

(4) Public review.

(A) In general. Any interested person may obtain review of an administrative penalty order issued under this subsection. The review may be obtained in the United States District Court for the District of Columbia or in the United States District Court for the district in which the violation is alleged to have occurred by the filing of a complaint with the court within the 30-day period beginning on the date the penalty order becomes final. The person filing the complaint shall simultaneously send a copy of the complaint by certified mail to the Administrator and the Attorney General.

(B) Record. The Administrator shall promptly file in the court a certified copy of the record on which the order was issued.

(C) Standard of review. The court shall not set aside or remand the order unless the court finds that there is not substantial evidence in the record, taken as a whole, to support the finding of a violation or that the assessment of the penalty by the Administrator constitutes an abuse of discretion.

(D) Prohibition on additional penalties. The court may not impose an additional civil penalty for a violation that is subject to the order unless the court finds that the assessment constitutes an abuse of discretion by the Administrator.

(c) Limitation on State use of funds collected from Federal Government. Unless a State law in effect on the date of enactment of the Safe Drinking Water Act Amendments of 1996 [enacted Aug. 6, 1996] or a State constitution requires the funds to be used in a different manner, all funds collected by a State from the Federal Government from penalties and fines imposed for violation of any substantive or procedural requirement referred to in subsection (a) shall be used by the State only for projects designed to improve or protect the environment or to defray the costs of environmental protection or enforcement.

(d) Indian rights and sovereignty as unaffected; "Federal agency" defined.

(1) Nothing in the Safe Drinking Water Amendments of 1977 shall be construed to alter or affect the status of American Indian lands or water rights nor to waive any sovereignty over Indian lands guaranteed by treaty or statute.

(2) For the purposes of this Act, the term "Federal agency" shall not be construed to refer to or include any American Indian tribe, nor to the Secretary of the Interior in his capacity as trustee of Indian lands.

(e) Washington Aqueduct. The Secretary of the Army shall not pass the cost of any penalty assessed under this title [42 USCS §§ 300f et seq.] on to any customer, user, or other purchaser of drinking water from the Washington Aqueduct system, including finished water from the Dalecarlia or McMillan treatment plant.

SECTION 300J-7. JUDICIAL REVIEW

(a) Courts of appeals; petition for review: actions respecting regulations; filing period; grounds arising after expiration of filing period; exclusiveness of remedy. A petition for review of—

(1) actions pertaining to the establishment of national primary drinking water regulations (including maximum contaminant level

goals) may be filed only in the United States Court of Appeals for the District of Columbia circuit; and

(2) any other final action of the Administrator under this Act may be filed in the circuit in which the petitioner resides or transacts business which is directly affected by the action.

Any such petition shall be filed within the 45-day period beginning on the date of the promulgation of the regulation or any final Agency action with respect to which review is sought or on the date of the determination with respect to which review is sought, and may be filed after the expiration of such 45-day period if the petition is based solely on grounds arising after the expiration of such period. Action of the Administrator with respect to which review could have been obtained under this subsection shall not be subject to judicial review in any civil or criminal proceeding for enforcement or in any civil action to enjoin enforcement. In any petition concerning the assessment of a civil penalty pursuant to section 1414(g)(3)(B) [42 USCS § 300g-3(g)(3)(B)], the petitioner shall simultaneously send a copy of the complaint by certified mail to the Administrator and the Attorney General. The court shall set aside and remand the penalty order if the court finds that there is not substantial evidence in the record to support the finding of a violation or that the assessment of the penalty by the Administrator constitutes an abuse of discretion.

(b) District courts; petition for review: actions respecting variances or exemptions; filing period; grounds arising after expiration of filing period; exclusiveness of remedy. The United States district courts shall have jurisdiction of actions brought to review (1) the granting of, or the refusing to grant, a variance or exemption under section 1415 or 1416 [42 USCS § 300g-4 or 300g-5] or (2) the requirements of any schedule prescribed for a variance or exemption under such section or the failure to prescribe such a schedule. Such an action may only be brought upon a petition for review filed with the court within the 45-day period beginning on the date the action sought to be reviewed is taken or, in the case of a petition to review the refusal to grant a variance or exemption or the failure to prescribe a schedule, within the 45-day period beginning on the date action is required to be taken on the variance, exemption, or schedule, as the case may be. A petition for such review may be filed after the expiration of such period if the petition is based solely on grounds arising after the expiration of such period. Action with respect to which review could have been obtained under this subsection shall not be subject to judicial review in any civil or criminal proceeding for enforcement or in any civil action to enjoin enforcement.

(c) Judicial order for additional evidence before Administrator; modified or new findings; recommendation for modification or setting aside of original determination. In any judicial proceeding in which review is sought of a determination under this title [42 USCS §§ 300f et seq.] required to be made on the record after notice and opportunity for hearing, if any party applies to the court for leave to adduce additional evidence and shows to the satisfaction of the court that such additional evidence is material and that there were reasonable grounds for the failure to adduce such evidence in the proceeding before the Administrator, the court may order such additional evidence (and evidence in rebuttal thereof) to be taken before the Administrator, in such manner and upon such terms and conditions as the court may deem proper. The Administrator may modify his findings as to the facts, or make new findings, by reason of the additional evidence so taken, and he shall file such modified or new findings, and his recommendation, if any, for the modification or setting aside of his original determination, with the return of such additional evidence.

300J-8. CITIZEN'S CIVIL ACTIONS

(a) Persons subject to civil actions; jurisdiction of enforcement proceedings. Except as provided in subsection (b) of this section, any person may commence a civil action on his own behalf—

(1) against any person (including (A) the United States, and (B) any other governmental instrumentality or agency to the extent permitted by the eleventh amendment to the Constitution) who is alleged to be in violation of any requirement prescribed by or under this title [42 USCS §§ 300f et seq.];

(2) against the Administrator where there is alleged a failure of the Administrator to perform any act or duty under this title [42 USCS §§ 300f et seq.] which is not discretionary with the Administrator; or

(3) for the collection of a penalty by the United States Government (and associated costs and interest) against any Federal agency that fails, by the date that is 18 months after the effective date of a final order to pay a penalty assessed by the Administrator under section 1429(b) [42 USCS § 300h-8], to pay the penalty.

No action may be brought under paragraph (1) against a public water system for a violation of a requirement prescribed by or under this title [42 USCS §§ 300f et seq.] which occurred within the 27-month period beginning on the first day of the month in which this title is enacted [enacted Dec. 16, 1974]. The United States district courts shall have jurisdiction, without regard to the amount in controversy or the citizenship of the parties, to enforce in an action brought under this subsection any requirement prescribed by or under this title [42 USCS §§ 300f et seq.] or to order the Administrator to perform an act or duty described in paragraph (2), as the case may be.

(b) Conditions for commencement of civil action; notice. No civil action may be commenced—

(1) under subsection (a)(1) of this section respecting violation of a requirement prescribed by or under this title [42 USCS §§ 300f et seq.]—

(A) prior to sixty days after the plaintiff has given notice of such violation (i) to the Administrator, (ii) to any alleged violator of such requirement and (iii) to the State in which the violation occurs, or

(B) if the Administrator, the Attorney General, or the State has commenced and is diligently prosecuting a civil action in a court of the United States to require compliance with such requirement, but in any such action in a court of the United States any person may intervene as a matter of right; or (2) under subsection (a)(2) of this section prior to sixty days after the plaintiff has given notice of such action to the Administrator; or (3) under subsection (a)(3) prior to 60 days after the plaintiff has given notice of such action to the Attorney General and to the Federal agency.

Notice required by this subsection shall be given in such manner as the Administrator shall prescribe by regulation. No person may commence a civil action under subsection (a) to require a State to prescribe a schedule under section 1415 or 1416 [42 USCS § 300g-4 or 300g-5] for a variance or exemption, unless such person shows to the satisfaction of the court that the State has in a substantial number of cases failed to prescribe such schedules.

(c) Intervention of right. In any action under this section, the Administrator or the Attorney General, if not a party, may intervene as a matter of right.

(d) Costs; attorney fees; expert witness fees; filing of bond. The court, in issuing any final order in any action brought under subsection (a) of this section, may award costs of litigation (including reasonable attorney and expert witness fees) to any party whenever the court determines such an award is appropriate. The court may, if a temporary restraining order or preliminary injunction is sought, require the filing of a bond or equivalent security in accordance with the Federal Rules of Civil Procedure.

(e) Availability of other relief. Nothing in this section shall restrict any right which any person (or class of persons) may have under any statute or common law to seek enforcement of any requirement prescribed by or under this title [42 USCS §§ 300f et seq.] or to seek any other relief. Nothing in this section or in any other law of the United States shall be construed to prohibit, exclude, or restrict any State or local government from—

(1) bringing any action or obtaining any remedy or sanction in any State or local court, or

(2) bringing any administrative action or obtaining any administrative remedy or sanction, against any agency of the United States under State or local law to enforce any requirement respecting the provision of safe drinking water or respecting any underground injection control program. Nothing in this section shall be construed to authorize judicial review of regulations or orders of the Administrator under this title [42 USCS §§ 300f et seq.], except as provided in section 1448 [42 USCS § 300j-7]. For provisions providing for application of certain requirements to such agencies in the same manner as to nongovernmental entities, see section 1447 [42 USCS § 300j-6].

APPENDIX 11:
DIRECTORY OF INTERNET ADDRESSES
FOR STATE UNDERGROUND STORAGE
TANK PROGRAMS

STATE	INTERNET ADDRESS
ALASKA	http://www.state.ak.us/dec/dspar/stp_home.htm
ALABAMA	http://www.adem.state.al.us/EnviroProtect/Water/Ground/grdwater.htm
ARKANSAS	http://www.adeq.state.ar.us/rst
ARIZONA	http://www.adeq.state.az.us/environ/waste/ust/index.html
CALIFORNIA	http://www.swrcb.ca.gov/cwphome/ust
COLORADO	http://oil.cdle.state.co.us
CONNECTICUT	http://www.dep.state.ct.us/wst/ust/indexust.htm
DISTRICT OF COLUMBIA	http://dchealth.dc.gov/services/administration_offices/environmental/services2/ustd/index.shtm
DELAWARE	http://www.dnrec.state.de.us/dnrec2000/divisions/awm/ust
FLORIDA	http://www.dep.state.fl.us/waste/categories/tanks/default.htm
GEORGIA	http://www.dnr.state.ga.us/dnr/environ
HAWAII	http://www.state.hi.us/doh/eh/shwb/ust/index.html
IOWA	http://www.state.ia.us/dnr/organiza/wmad/lqbureau/ust/index.htm
IDAHO	http://www2.state.id.us/deq/waste/waste1.htm
ILLINOIS	http://www.state.il.us/osfm/prepcs.htm
INDIANA	http://www.state.in.us/idem/olq/about_olq/programs.html#ust

STATE	INTERNET ADDRESS
KANSAS	http://www.kdhe.state.ks.us/tanks
KENTUCKY	http://www.nr.state.ky.us/nrepc/dep/waste/programs/ust/usthome.htm
LOUISIANA	http://www.deq.state.la.us/remediation/index.htm
MASSACHUSETTS	http://www.state.ma.us/dfs/ust/usthome.htm
MARYLAND	http://www.mde.state.md.us/reference/factsheets/oil control.html
MICHIGAN	http://www.deq.state.mi.us/std/index.html
MINNESOTA	http://www.pca.state.mn.us/cleanup/ust.html
MISSOURI	http://www.dnr.state.mo.us/deq/hwp/tanks.htm
MISSISSIPPI	http://www.deq.state.ms.us/newweb/homepages.nsf
MONTANA	http://www.deq.state.mt.us/rem/tsb/ess/ess.asp
NORTH CAROLINA	http://ust.enr.state.nc.us
NORTH DAKOTA	http://www.ehs.health.state.nd.us/ndhd/environ/wm/ust
NEBRASKA	http://vmhost.cdp.state.ne.us:97/~sfmweb/sfmhome.html
NEW HAMPSHIRE	http://www.des.state.nh.us/orcb/ustprog.htm
NEW JERSEY	http://www.state.nj.us/dep/srp/bust/bust.htm
NEW MEXICO	http://www.nmenv.state.nm.us/ust/ustbtop.html
NEVADA	http://ndep.state.nv.us/bca/ust_home.htm
NEW YORK	http://www.dec.state.ny.us/website/der
OHIO	https://www.com.state.oh.us/odoc/sfm/bustr/default2.asp
OKLAHOMA	http://www.occ.state.ok.us/text_files/ustdead.htm
OREGON	http://www.deq.state.or.us/wmc/tank/ust-lust.htm
PENNSYLVANIA	http://www.dep.state.pa.us/dep/deputate/airwaste/wm/tanks/storagetanks
RHODE ISLAND	http://www.dem.state.ri.us/dem_wastemgt/ust/usthome.htm
SOUTH CAROLINA	http://www.scdhec.net/ust
SOUTH DAKOTA	http://www.state.sd.us/state/executive/denr/des/ground/groundprg.htm
TENNESSEE	http://www.state.tn.us/environment/ust
TEXAS	http://www.tnrcc.state.tx.us/permitting/r_e/pstta
UTAH	http://www.eq.state.ut.us/eqerr/errhmpg.htm

STATE	INTERNET ADDRESS
VIRGINIA	http://www.deq.state.va.us/tanks
VERMONT	http://www.anr.state.vt.us/dec/wastediv/sms/smsgdint.htm
WASHINGTON	http://www.ecy.wa.gov/programs/tcp/ust-lust/tanks.html
WISCONSIN	http://www.commerce.state.wi.us/er/er-bst-homepage.html
WYOMING	http://deq.state.wy.us/wqd/tankpg.htm

SOURCE: U.S. Environmental Protection Agency

APPENDIX 12:
U.S. ENVIRONMENTAL PROTECTION
AGENCY—WETLANDS
DIVISION—REGIONAL OFFICES

REGION	AREAS COVERED	ADDRESS	TELEPHONE	FAX
Headquarters	Overall	U.S. EPA—Wetlands Division, 401 M Street SW, Washington, DC 20460	(202) 260-7791	(202) 260-2356
Region I	CT, MA, ME, MH, RI, VT	U.S. EPA—Wetlands Division—Region I, John F. Kennedy Federal Building, Boston, MA 02203-1911	(617) 565-4421	(617) 565-4940
Region II	NJ, NY, PR, VI	U.S. EPA—Wetlands Division—Region II, 26 Federal Plaza, Room 837, New York, NY 10278	(212) 264-5170	(212) 264-4690

REGION	AREAS COVERED	ADDRESS	TELEPHONE	FAX
Region III	DE, MD, PA, VA, WV	U.S. EPA—Wetlands Division—Region III, 841 Chestnut Street, Philadelphia, PA 19107	(215) 597-9301	(215) 597-1850
Region IV	AL, FL, GA, KY, MS, NC, SC, TN	U.S. EPA—Wetlands Division—Region IV, 345 Courtland Street, N.E., Atlanta, GA 30365	(404) 347-4015	(404) 347-3269
Region V	IL, IN, MI, MN, OH, WI	U.S. EPA—Wetlands Division—Region V, 77 West Jackson Boulevard, Chicago, IL 60604	(312) 886-0243	(312) 886-7804
Region VI	AR, LA, NM, OK, TX	U.S. EPA—Wetlands Division—Region VI, 1445 Ross Avenue, Suite 900, Dallas, TX 75202	(214) 655-2263	(214) 655-7446
Region VII	IA, KS, MO, NE	U.S. EPA—Wetlands Division—Region VII, 726 Minnesota Avenue, Kansas City, KS 66101	(913) 551-7540	(913) 551-7863

REGION	AREAS COVERED	ADDRESS	TELEPHONE	FAX
Region VIII	CO, MT, ND, SD, UT, WY	U.S. EPA—Wetlands Division—Region VIII, 999 18th Street, 500 Denver Place, Denver, CO 80202-2405	(303) 293-1570	(303) 391-6957
Region IX	AZ, CA, HI, NV, Pacific Islands	U.S. EPA—Wetlands Division—Region IX, 75 Hawthorne Street, San Francisco, CA 94105	(415) 744-1968	(415) 744-1078
Region X	AK, ID, OR, WA	U.S. EPA—Wetlands Division—Region X, 1200 Sixth Avenue, Seattle, WA 98101	(206) 553-1412	(206) 553-1775

SOURCE: U.S. Environmental Protection Agency, Wetlands Division

GLOSSARY

Abatement—Reducing the degree or intensity of, or eliminating, pollution.

Accident Site—The location of an unexpected occurrence, failure or loss, either at a plant or along a transportation route, resulting in a release of hazardous materials.

Acclimatization—The physiological and behavioral adjustments of an organism to changes in its environment.

Acid Aerosol—Acidic liquid or solid particles that are small enough to become airborne. High concentrations of acid aerosols can be irritating to the lungs and have been associated with some respiratory diseases, such as asthma.

Acid Rain—A complex chemical and atmospheric phenomenon that occurs when emissions of sulfur and nitrogen compounds and other substances are transformed by chemical processes in the atmosphere, often far from the original sources, and then deposited on earth in either wet or dry form. The wet forms, popularly called "acid rain," can fall as rain, snow, or fog. The dry forms are acidic gases or particulates.

Acidic—The condition of water or soil that contains a sufficient amount of acid substances to lower the pH below 7.0

Active Ingredient—In any pesticide product, the component that kills, or otherwise controls, target pests.

Acute Toxicity—The ability of a substance to cause poisonous effects resulting in severe biological harm or death soon after a single exposure or dose.

Adaptation—Changes in an organism's structure or habits that help it adjust to its surroundings.

Administrative Order—A legal document signed by EPA directing an individual, business, or other entity to take corrective action or refrain from an activity.

Administrative Procedures Act—A law that spells out procedures and requirements related to the promulgation of regulations.

Aeration—A process which promotes biological degradation of organic matter in water.

Aeration Tank—A chamber used to inject air into water.

Aerosol—A suspension of liquid or solid particles in a gas.

Affected Public—The people who live and/or work near a hazardous waste site.

Agricultural Pollution—Farming wastes, including runoff and leaching of pesticides and fertilizers; erosion and dust from plowing; improper disposal of animal manure and carcasses; crop residues, and debris.

Air Contaminant—Any particulate matter, gas, or combination thereof, other than water vapor.

Air Pollutant—Any substance in air that could, in high enough concentration, harm man, other animals, vegetation, or material.

Air Pollution Control Device—Mechanism or equipment that cleans emissions generated by an incinerator by removing pollutants that would otherwise be released to the atmosphere.

Air Pollution—The presence of contaminant or pollutant substances in the air that do not disperse properly and interfere with human health or welfare, or produce other harmful environmental effects.

Air Quality Criteria—The levels of pollution and lengths of exposure above which adverse health and welfare effects may occur.

Air Toxins—Any air pollutant for which a national ambient air quality standard (NAAQS) does not exist that may reasonably be anticipated to cause cancer, developmental effects, reproductive dysfunctions, neurological disorders, heritable gene mutations, or other serious or irreversible chronic or acute health effects in humans.

Airborne Particulates—Total suspended particulate matter found in the atmosphere as solid particles or liquid droplets.

Airborne Release—Release of any chemical into the air.

Algae—Simple rootless plants that grow in sunlit waters in proportion to the amount of available nutrients. They can affect water quality adversely by lowering the dissolved oxygen in the water.

Alkaline—The condition of water or soil which contains a sufficient amount of alkali substance to raise the pH above 7.0.

Alkalinity—The capacity of water to neutralize acids.

Allergen—A substance capable of causing an allergic reaction because of an individual's sensitivity to that substance.

Allergic Rhinitis—Inflammation of the mucous membranes in the nose that is caused by an allergic reaction.

Alternative Fuels—Substitutes for traditional liquid, oil-derived motor vehicle fuels like gasoline and diesel. Includes methanol, ethanol, compressed natural gas, and others.

Ambient Air—Any unconfined portion of the atmosphere—open air, surrounding air.

Animal Dander—Tiny scales of animal skin.

Aquifer—An underground geological formation, or group of formations, containing usable amounts of groundwater that can supply wells and springs.

Asbestos—A mineral fiber that can pollute air or water and cause cancer or asbestosis when inhaled.

Asbestosis—A disease associated with inhalation of asbestos fibers. The disease makes breathing progressively more difficult and can be fatal.

Assay—A test for a particular chemical or effect.

Assimilation—The ability of a body of water to purify itself of pollutants.

Attainment Area—An area considered to have air quality as good as or better than the national ambient air quality standards as defined in the Clean Air Act.

Background Level—In air pollution control, the concentration of air pollutants in a definite area during a fixed period of time prior to the starting up or on the stoppage of a source of emission under control.

Bacteria—Microscopic living organisms that can aid in pollution control by metabolizing organic matter in sewage, oil spills or other pollutants. However, bacteria in soil, water or air can also cause human, animal and plant health problems.

BEN—EPA's computer model for analyzing a violator's economic gain from not complying with the law.

Biodegradable—Capable of decomposing rapidly under natural conditions.

Biological Control—In pest control, the use of animals and organisms that eat or otherwise kill or out-compete pests.

Biological Treatment—A treatment technology that uses bacteria to consume organic waste.

Biomass—All of the living material in a given area; often refers to vegetation.

Biosphere—The portion of Earth and its atmosphere that can support life.

Biotic Community—A naturally occurring assemblage of plants and animals that live in the same environment and are mutually sustaining and interdependent.

Blackwater—Water that contains animal, human, or food waste.

Blood Products—Any product derived from human blood, including but not limited to blood plasma, platelets, red or white corpuscles, and derived licensed products such as interferon.

Bog—A type of wetland that accumulates appreciable peat deposits. Bogs depend primarily on precipitation for their water source, and are usually acidic and rich in plant residue with a conspicuous mat of living green moss.

Bottom Land Hardwoods—Forested freshwater wetlands adjacent to rivers in the southeastern United States, especially valuable for wildlife breeding, nesting and habitat.

Building-Related Illness—A discrete, identifiable disease or illness that can be traced to a specific pollutant or source within a building.

Burial Ground—A disposal site for radioactive waste materials that uses earth or water as a shield.

Cap—A layer of clay, or other impermeable material installed over the top of a closed landfill to prevent entry of rainwater and minimize leachate.

Capacity Assurance Plan—A statewide plan which supports a state's ability to manage the hazardous waste generated within its boundaries over a twenty year period.

Carbon Monoxide (CO)—A colorless, odorless, poisonous gas produced by incomplete fossil fuel combustion.

Carcinogen—Any substance that can cause or aggravate cancer.

Characteristic—Any one of the four categories used in defining hazardous waste—ignitability, corrosivity, reactivity, and toxicity.

Chemical Sensitization—Evidence suggests that some people may develop health problems characterized by effects such as dizziness, eye and throat irritation, chest tightness, and nasal congestion that appear whenever they are exposed to certain chemicals. People may react to even trace amounts of chemicals to which they have become "sensitized."

Chemical Treatment—Any one of a variety of technologies that use chemicals or a variety of chemical processes to treat waste.

Chlorinated Hydrocarbons—These include a class of persistent, broad-spectrum insecticides that linger in the environment and accumulate in the food chain.

Chlorination—The application of chlorine to drinking water, sewage, or industrial waste to disinfect or to oxidize undesirable compounds.

Chlorofluorocarbons (CFCs)—A family of inert, nontoxic, and easily liquified chemicals used in refrigeration, air conditioning, packaging, insulation, or as solvents and aerosol propellants.

Chronic Toxicity—The capacity of a substance to cause long-term poisonous human health effects.

Clarifier—A tank in which solids settle to the bottom and are subsequently removed as sludge.

Clean Fuels—Blends or substitutes for gasoline fuels, including compressed natural gas, methanol, ethanol, liquified petroleum gas, and others.

Cleanup—Actions taken to deal with a release or threat of release of a hazardous substance that could affect humans and/or the environment.

Coliform Index—A rating of the purity of water based on a count of fecal bacteria.

Coliform Organism—Microorganisms found in the intestinal tract of humans and animals.

Commercial Waste—All solid wastes emanating from business establishments such as stores, markets, office buildings, restaurants, shopping centers, and theaters.

Decontamination—Removal of harmful substances such as noxious chemicals, harmful bacteria or other organisms, or radioactive material from exposed individuals, rooms and furnishings in buildings, or the exterior environment.

Deep-Well Injection—Deposition of raw or treated, filtered hazardous waste by pumping it into deep wells, where it is contained in the pores of permeable subsurface rock.

Defluoridation—The removal of excess fluoride in drinking water to prevent the staining of teeth.

Defoliant—An herbicide that removes leaves from trees and growing plants.

DES—A synthetic estrogen, diethylstilbestrol is used as a growth stimulant in food animals. Residues in meat are thought to be carcinogenic.

Designated Pollutant—An air pollutant which is neither a criteria nor hazardous pollutant, as described in the Clean Air Act, but for which new source performance standards exist.

Direct Runoff—Water that flows over the ground surface or through the ground directly into streams, rivers, and lakes.

Ecological Impact—The effect that a man-made or natural activity has on living organisms and their non-living environment.

Ecology—The relationship of living things to one another and their environment, or the study of such relationships.

Emission—Pollution discharged into the atmosphere from smoke-stacks, other vents, and surface areas of commercial or industrial facilities; from residential chimneys; and from motor vehicle, locomotive, or aircraft exhausts.

Emission Standard—The maximum amount of air polluting discharge legally allowed from a single source, mobile or stationary.

Endangered Species—Animals, birds, fish, plants, or other living organisms threatened with extinction by man-made or natural changes in their environment.

Environmental Impact Statement—A document required of federal agencies by the National Environmental Policy Act for major projects or legislative proposals significantly affecting the environment.

Environmental Justice—The fair treatment of all races, cultures, incomes, and educational levels with respect to the development, implementation, and enforcement of environmental laws, regulations, and policies.

Environmental Tobacco Smoke (ETS)—Mixture of smoke from the burning end of a cigarette, pipe, or cigar and smoke exhaled by the smoker (also known as secondhand smoke).

Feasibility Study—Analysis of the practicability of a proposal.

Fecal Coliform Bacteria—Bacteria found in the intestinal tracts of mammals. Their presence in water or sludge is an indicator of pollution and possible contamination by pathogens.

Fen—A type of wetland that accumulates peat deposits. Fens are less acidic than bogs, deriving most of their water from groundwater rich in calcium and magnesium.

FIFRA Pesticide Ingredient—An ingredient of a pesticide that must be registered with EPA under the Federal Insecticide, fungicide, and Rodenticide Act.

Floodplain—The flat or nearly flat land along a river or stream or in a tidal area that is covered by water during a flood.

Fluoridation—The addition of a chemical to increase the concentration of fluoride ions drinking water to reduce the incidence of tooth decay in children.

Fluorocarbons (FCs)—Any of a number of organic compounds analogous to hydrocarbons in which one or more hydrogen atoms are replaced by fluorine.

Fossil Fuel—Fuel derived from ancient organic remains, e.g., peat, coal, crude oil, and natural gas.

Fresh Water—Water that generally contains less than 1,000 milligrams-per liter of dissolved solids.

Fungi—Any of a group of parasitic lower plants that lack chlorophyll, including molds and mildews.

Fungicide—Pesticides which are used to control, deter, or destroy fungi.

Grab Sample—A single sample collected at a particular time and place that represents the composition of the water only at that time and place.

Greenhouse Effect—The warming of the Earth's atmosphere attributed to a build-up of carbon dioxide or other gases.

Ground Water—The supply of fresh water found beneath the Earth's surface, usually in aquifers, which supply wells and springs.

Habitat—The place where a population (e.g., human, animal, plant, microorganism) lives and its surroundings, both living and non-living.

Hazardous Air Pollutants—Air pollutants which are not covered by ambient air quality standards but which, as defined in the Clean Air Act, may reasonably be expected to cause or contribute to irreversible illness or death.

Hazardous Substance—Any material that poses a threat to human health and/or the environment.

Hazardous Waste—By-products of society that can pose a substantial or potential hazard to human health or the environment when improperly managed.

Health Advisory Level—A non-regulatory health-based reference level of chemical traces in drinking water at which there are no adverse health risks when ingested over various periods of time.

Humidifier Fever—A respiratory illness caused by exposure to toxins from microorganisms found in wet or moist areas in humidifiers and air conditioners. Also called air conditioner or ventilation fever.

Hydrocarbons (HC)—Chemical compounds that consist entirely of carbon and hydrogen.

Hypersensitivity Pneumonitis—A group of respiratory diseases that cause inflammation of the lung. Most forms of hypersensitivity pneumonitis are caused by the inhalation of organic dusts, including molds.

Incidental Taking —An unintentional, but not unexpected, taking.

Indoor Air Pollution—Chemical, physical, or biological contaminants in indoor air.

Infectious Waste—Hazardous waste with infectious characteristics, including—contaminated animal waste; human blood and blood products; isolation waste, pathological waste; and discarded sharps instruments.

Landfills—Sanitary disposal sites for non-hazardous solid wastes spread in layers, compacted to the smallest practical volume, and covered by material applied at the end of each operating day. Secure chemical landfills are disposal sites for hazardous waste, selected and designed to minimize the chance of release of hazardous substances into the environment.

Mandatory Recycling—Programs which by law require consumers to separate trash so that some or all recyclable materials are recovered for recycling rather than going to landfills.

Maximum Contaminant Level—The maximum permissible level of a contaminant in water delivered to any user of a public system.

Mitigation—Measures taken to reduce adverse impacts on the environment.

Mobile Source—Any non-stationary source of air pollution such as cars, trucks, motorcycles, buses, airplanes, locomotives.

Morbidity—Rate of disease incidence.

National Ambient Air Quality Standards (NAAQS)—Standards established by EPA that apply for outside air throughout the country.

National Pollutant Discharge Elimination System (NPDES)—A provision of the Clean Water Act which prohibits discharge of pollutants into waters of the United States unless a special permit is issued by EPA, a state, or, where delegated, a tribal government on an Indian reservation.

National Response Team (NRT)—Representatives of 13 federal agencies that, as a team, coordinate federal responses to nationally significant incidents of pollution—an oil spill, a major chemical release, or a Superfund response action—and provide advice and technical assistance to the responding agency(ies) before and during a response action.

Navigable Waters—Traditionally, waters sufficiently deep and wide for navigation by all, or specified vessels; such waters in the United States come under federal jurisdiction and are protected by certain provisions of the Clean Water Act.

NOx—Product of combustion from transportation and stationary sources and a major contributor to the formation of ozone in the troposphere and to acid deposition.

Non-Attainment Area—Area that does not meet one or more of the National Ambient Air Quality Standards for the criteria pollutants designated in the Clean Air Act.

Oil Spill—An accidental or intentional discharge of oil which reaches bodies of water.

Organic Compounds—Chemicals that contain carbon. Volatile organic compounds vaporize at room temperature and pressure. They are found in many indoor sources, including many common household products and building materials.

Ozone Hole—Thinning break in the stratospheric ozone layer.

Ozone Layer—The protective layer in the atmosphere, about 15 miles above the ground, that absorbs some of the sun's ultraviolet rays, thereby reducing the amount of potentially harmful radiation reaching the earth's surface.

Particulates—Fine liquid or solid particles such as dust, smoke, mist, fumes, or smog found in air or emissions.

Permit—An authorization, license, or equivalent control document issued by EPA or an approved state agency to implement the requirements of an environmental regulation.

Pesticide—Substances or mixture there of intended for preventing, destroying, repelling, or mitigating any pest.

pH—An expression of the intensity of the basic or acid condition of a liquid.

Picocurie (pCi)—A unit for measuring radioactivity, often expressed as picocuries per liter (pCi/L) of air.

Pollutant—Generally, any substance introduced into the environment that adversely affects the usefulness of a resource.

Pollutant Standard Index (PSI)—Measure of adverse health effects of air pollution levels in major cities.

Pollution—Generally, the presence of matter or energy whose nature, location, or quantity produces undesired environmental effects.

Polyvinyl Chloride (PVC)—A tough, environmentally indestructible plastic that releases hydrochloric acid when burned.

Pressed Wood Products—A group of materials used in building and furniture construction that are made from wood veneers, particles, or fibers bonded together with an adhesive under heat and pressure.

Primary Drinking Water Regulation—Applies to public water systems and specifies a contaminant level, which, in the judgment of the EPA Administrator, will not adversely affect human health.

Radon (Rn)—Radon is a radioactive gas formed in the decay of uranium.

Radon Decay Products—Radon decay products (also called radon daughters or progeny) can be breathed into the lung where they continue to release radiation as they further decay.

Raw Sewage—Untreated wastewater and its contents.

Recommended Maximum Contaminant Level (RMCL)—The maximum level of a contaminant in drinking water at which no known or anticipated adverse affect on human health would occur.

Recycle—Minimizing waste generation by recovering and reprocessing usable products that might otherwise become waste.

Regional Response Team (RRT)—Representatives of federal, local, and state agencies who may assist in coordination of activities at the request of the On-Scene Coordinator before and during a significant pollution incident such as an oil spill, major chemical release, or a Superfund response.

Release—Any spilling, leaking, pumping, pouring, emitting, emptying, discharging, injecting, escaping, leaching, dumping, or disposing into the environment of a hazardous or toxic chemical or extremely hazardous substance.

Reportable Quantity (RQ)—Quantity of a hazardous substance that triggers reports under CERCLA.

Risk—A measure of the probability that damage to life, health, property, and/or the environment will occur as a result of a given hazard.

Salt Water Intrusion—The invasion of fresh surface or ground water by salt water.

Salvage—The utilization of waste materials.

Secondary Drinking Water Regulations—Non-enforceable regulations applying to public water systems and specifying the maximum contamination levels that, in the judgment of EPA, are required to protect the public welfare.

Septic Tank—An underground storage tank for wastes from homes not connected to a sewer line. Waste goes directly from the home to the tank.

Serious Injury —Any injury that will likely result in mortality.

Sewage—The waste and wastewater produced by residential and commercial sources and discharged into sewers.

Sewer—A channel or conduit that carries wastewater and storm-water runoff from the source to a treatment plant or receiving stream.

Sick Building Syndrome—Term that refers to a set of symptoms that affect some number of building occupants during the time they spend in the building and diminish or go away during periods when they leave the building. Cannot be traced to specific pollutants or sources within the building.

Smog—Air pollution associated with oxidants.

Solid Waste Management—Supervised handling of waste materials from their source through recovery processes to disposal.

State Emergency Response Commission (SERC)—Commission appointed by each state governor according to the requirements of SARA Title III.

State Implementation Plans (SIP)—EPA approved state plans for the establishment, regulation, and enforcement of air pollution standards.

Stationary Source—A fixed-site producer of pollution, mainly power plants and other facilities using industrial combustion processes.

Storm Sewer—A system of pipes that carries only water runoff from buildings and land surfaces.

Strip-Mining—A process that uses machines to scrape soil or rock away from mineral deposits just under the earth's surface.

Subsistence—The use of marine mammals taken by Alaskan Natives for food, clothing, shelter, heating, transportation, and other uses necessary to maintain the life of the taker or those who depend upon the taker to provide them with such subsistence.

Superfund—The program operated under the legislative authority of CERCLA and SARA that funds and carries out EPA solid waste emergency and long-term removal and remedial activities.

Surface Runoff—Precipitation, snow melt, or irrigation in excess of what can infiltrate the soil surface and be stored in small surface depressions; a major transporter of nonpoint source pollutants.

Toxic Substance—A chemical or mixture that may present an unreasonable risk of injury to health or the environment.

Toxic Waste—A waste that can produce injury if inhaled, swallowed, or absorbed through the skin.

Treated Wastewater—Wastewater that has been subjected to one or more physical, chemical, and biological processes to reduce its pollution of health hazards.

Treatment Plant—A structure built to treat wastewater before discharging it into the environment.

Trust Fund (CERCLA)—A fund set up under the Comprehensive Environmental Response, Compensation and Liability Act (CERCLA) to help pay for cleanup of hazardous waste sites and for legal action to force those responsible for the sites to clean them up.

Ultraviolet Rays—Radiation from the sun that can be useful or potentially harmful. UV rays from one part of the spectrum (UV-A) enhance plant life and are useful in some medical and dental procedures; UV rays from other parts of the spectrum (UV-B) can cause skin cancer or other tissue damage.

Underground Injection Control (UIC)—The program under the Safe Drinking Water Act that regulates the use of wells to pump fluids into the ground.

Underground Storage Tank—A tank located at least partially underground and designed to hold gasoline or other petroleum products or chemicals.

Urban Runoff—Storm water from city streets and adjacent domestic or commercial properties that carries pollutants of various kinds into the sewer systems and receiving waters.

Ventilation Rate—The rate at which indoor air enters and leaves a building. Expressed in one of two ways—the number of changes of outdoor air per unit of time (air changes per hour, or "ach") or the rate at which a volume of outdoor air enters per unit of time (cubic feet per minute, or "cfm").

Volatile Organic Compound (VOC)—Any organic compound that participates in atmospheric photochemical reactions except those designated by EPA as having negligible photochemical reactivity.

Waste—Unwanted materials left over from a manufacturing process or refuse from places of human or animal habitation.

Wastewater—The spent or used water from a home, community, farm, or industry that contains dissolved or suspended matter.

Water Pollution—The presence in water of enough harmful or objectionable material to damage the water's quality.

Watershed—The land area that drains into a stream; the watershed for a major river may encompass a number of smaller watersheds that ultimately combine at a common delivery point.

Zooplankton—Tiny aquatic animals eaten by fish.

SOURCE: U.S. ENVIRONMENTAL PROTECTION AGENCY

BIBLIOGRAPHY AND ADDITIONAL READING

The Alliance to End Childhood Lead Poisoning (Date Visited: January 2002) <http://www.aeclp.org>.

The American Lung Association (Date Visited: January 2002) <http://www.lungusa.org/air>.

Bregman, Jacob I. and Mackenthun, Kenneth M. *Environmental Regulations Handbook*. Boca Raton, FL: Lewis Publishing Company, 1992.

The Centers for Disease Control (Date Visited: January 2002) <http://www.cdc.gov>.

The Environmental Defense Fund (Date Visited: January 2002) <http://www.scorecard.org>.

The Environmental Protection Agency (Date Visited: January 2002) <http://www.epa.gov>.

The Environmental Protection Agency Air Pollution Standard Index (Date Visited: January 2002) <http://www.epa.gov/airnow>.

The Environmental Protection Agency Office of Air and Radiation/Office of Air Quality Planning and Standards (Date Visited: January 2002) <http://www.epa.gov/oar/oaqps>.

The Environmental Protection Agency Office of Children's Health Protection (Date Visited: January 2002) <http://www.epa.gov/children>.

The Environmental Protection Agency Safewater Website (Date Visited: January 2002)<http://www.epa.gov/safewater>.

Miller, Jeffrey G. *Citizen Suits: Private Enforcement of Federal Pollution Control Laws*. New York, NY: Wiley Law Publications, 1987.

Reitze, Arnold W. *Air Pollution Law*. Charlottesville, VA: Michie Butterworth Publishing Company, 1995.

Vaughan, Ray *Essentials of Environmental Law*. Rockville, MD: Government Institutes, 1994.

The Weather Channel (Date Visited: January 2002) <http://www.weather.com/health/airquality>.